LEARNINGAMES
for the
FIRST THREE YEARS

LEARNINGAMES
FOR THE FIRST
THREE YEARS

A GUIDE TO PARENT/CHILD PLAY

Joseph Sparling and Isabelle Lewis

Frank Porter Graham Child Development Center
University of North Carolina at Chapel Hill

 **WALKER AND COMPANY • NEW YORK**

for Eleanor Richardson, our co-worker, who has taught us much and whose love for all young children we respect

Copyright © 1978 by Frank Porter Graham Child Development Center
Copyright © 1979 by Joseph Sparling and Isabelle Lewis

First published in the United States of America in 1979 by the Walker Publishing Company, Inc.

Published simultaneously in Canada by John Wiley & Sons Canada, Limited, Rexdale, Ontario.

This paperback edition first published in 1984.

ISBN: 0-8027-7239-0

Library of Congress Catalog Card Number: 79-52624

Photography by Marilyn Peterson

Designed by Joyce C. Weston

Developmental research support for the curriculum on which the Learningames are based was supplied in part by a grant from the National Institute for Child Health and Human Development. Refinement and field testing were supported in part by Appalachian Regional Commission funds. Film for some of the pictures was supplied by the Polaroid Corporation. The material presented in this book does not necessarily reflect the educational philosophy of the sponsors and no official endorsement should be inferred.

Printed in the United States of America
10 9 8 7 6 5 4 3

ACKNOWLEDGMENTS

Are the ideas and activities suggested in the Learningames new? Very few of them. We have tried to collect some of the good practices that have been used for years by thoughtful parents, so some of the ideas will be very familiar to you. We've taken the trouble to write them down because they are important—even though they are simple and some are familiar. Recently, the child development theory of the Swiss psychologist Jean Piaget and the infant/parent programs of the American educator Ira Gordon also have become so familiar that they seem like "common knowledge." Almost everyone who has worked with infants in recent times has been influenced by these two pioneers, and we would like to gratefully acknowledge our obvious debt.

We would like to express our admiration for the foresight and leadership of the Child Development Section, Division of Plans and Operations (North Carolina Department of Human Resources) in bringing an earlier edition of Learningames into being as a part of their program development effort for the state of North Carolina—with the generous intention of releasing it to the national public.

The Learningames were produced in the Frank Porter Graham Child Development Center at the University of North Carolina at Chapel Hill. This center has been providing day care for infants since 1966. The parents and infants taught us a lot during this time. The careteachers in our center have also contributed many excellent ideas, as have our research assistants, who made hundreds of observations that helped us improve the games. Also, we want to recognize the special contribution of Ruth Wright, the first educational program director in the center, who wrote down some of the early ideas for these games and greatly stimulated our thinking.

We would like to say thank you for the enthusiastic participation of the staff and children of the Cleveland Avenue Child Development Center, where the Learningames were refined, and to acknowledge the creative contribution of the following staff members of the Frank Porter Graham Child Development Center, where the games originated.

Careteachers
Bettye Burnette
Susan Byrum
Eva Caldwell
Johnnie Cates
Janice Chevalier
Fannie Edwards
Lunary Edwards
Ruth Farrington
Jane Hall
Wanda Hunter
Annie Johnson
Eva Minor
Claire Pratt
Eleanor Richardson

Josephine Riggsbee
Tom Richey
Mary Rutala
Susan Stephan

Research Assistants
Ceil Coons
Paul Hirschbiel
Wain Mengal
Carolyn O'Brien

Secretaries
Nancy Hatley
Pat Roos
Mary Watkins

Administrators
Carrie Bynum
Lee Cross
Margaret Holmberg
Annie Pegram
Ruth Wright

Graduate Assistants
Karen Ehrmman
Frances Kendall
Pam Mills
Joan Parkinson
Janice Wheelon

Clearly, the authors feel they are sharing knowledge from many people and many sources. We hope that each reader will add his or her own insights, deepening and broadening the ideas in the Learningames.

Contents

Introduction

Many people used to believe that important learning begins when a child enters elementary school. But it is now becoming clear that the real beginning comes much earlier. What we have thought of as "only child's play" turns out to be very important. In fact, a child who does not have varied opportunities to learn and explore in infancy and early childhood starts the first grade at a distinct disadvantage—a disadvantage that may stay with him for years. Opportunities for early learning and opportunities for play go hand in hand, since learning for the very young child happens best through playful, gamelike activity. Nature is on our side. How fortunate that the things that will have an important payoff in the child's later ability to learn are the very things that are likely to be enjoyable for the infant and for the adult.

This is where the Learningames come in. The games are one-hundred experiences a child can enjoy from birth to thirty-six months of developmental age. In most of the Learningames an infant and adult are interacting—and learning as they have fun. Yes, they **both** learn. For example, while the baby is learning to reach and grasp, the adult may be learning to be a good observer or to select toys more wisely. Some readers will wish to select just a few games for their own use. Others will choose to use the activities systematically and frequently—making the games a curriculum or educational program. The Learningames are provided simply as a resource for child development. Hopefully, the uses parents and day care centers make of this resource will reflect the healthy variety that exists and should exist in parental goals.

Using the Learningames

These games are for parents, the natural teachers of their children. They are also for people who are preparing for parenthood and for professionals who have responsibility for very young children in day care or other types of child and family programs. Each game is presented on a double-page spread so that it can be found quickly and used easily. Some of the activities won't seem much like "games" at first sight, but we've called all of them games to emphasize the fact that they go best in a playful, back-and-forth exchange. The most important thing you can do to make these games succeed is to adopt the child's attitude that playing is the best way to learn.

What kinds of information are provided in each game?

The double-page description of the game provides information in brief, ready-reference style on the right-hand page and in greater detail on the left. Each side is divided into two main sections. The first section on each side tells how to play the game and the second section tells why.

The HOW section first describes what the adult does. The right-hand page will help you get a brief idea of the game's contents before going to the left for a closer reading. (This is not the usual sequence or direction for reading, but it puts all the "quick reading" on the convenient right-hand side.) Also on the right are one or two photographs of people engaged in playing the game. These photos were chosen to help you understand a particular action more clearly or to show an appropriate object or toy. In some of the games the adult is a male and in others a female. Helping a child grow is a job for both parents and for day care workers of both sexes.

On the left-hand page the how section describes, also, the responses infants usually make to the adult's action. The adult will want to give encouragement and praise when he sees these expected behaviors in the child. The response written for the baby is based on our experiences and is more a prediction of what the baby may do than a promise that he will. Babies have individual likes and dislikes. If your baby does not like a particular game, it makes sense to change the game so that it interests him more or to go on to another one.

The WHY section on each side of the double-page spread tries to give reasons for playing the game. We believe that if you know the reasoning behind a particular game, you'll be more able to invent other games or variations. And some games seem so simple that their importance may be overlooked—so we have tried to say why we think they're worth playing. On the right-hand page the why section gives the goal for your own behavior. This information is expanded on the left, and the uses of the baby's new skill are given. By knowing how the baby can put a new skill to use to master an even more difficult skill (sometimes one that is only weeks away and sometimes one that won't be learned for years to come), we can appreciate each simple bit of learning as a building block for the future.

Of course, whether your child masters skills in the future depends on many more things than these games. But when a baby has been given many opportunities to stretch and explore through Learningames, the parents or careteachers can feel that they've used one tested method for laying the foundation for the baby's future learning.

How are the games arranged?

Each of the six sections spans about a half-year of developmental age and begins with a short description of what to expect during this time. The games are arranged within each section in approximate order of increasing difficulty. This is meant to make it possible for the child and you to move easily through the games—not using every one but choosing those that are interesting to. the two of you. You will be experiencing a developmental progression as you move along. Even with picking and choosing on the basis of interest, you are likely to select a broad spectrum of types of games. If you are interested or concerned about types, each section's table of contents classifies the major child skill of each game under some aspect of social/emotional or intellectual/creative development. Of course, these classifications or themes don't tell the whole story because each game teaches more than one major skill. (For example, a game may be classified under the visual-motor theme but may also teach language, independence, and creativity.) Still, the major classification will help those parents who seek out particular types of games or who wish to keep track of their random choices.

Which children will benefit from the games?

Learningames are for any child who is developmentally under thirty-six months of age. This includes most children under age three and some normal and developmentally delayed children who are a little older. These games are not specifically designed for poor kids or rich kids, fast kids or slow kids—they can work for any child whose parents value the games and adapt them to the particular needs of the child. The games are not complete enough perhaps for some handicapped children, but they may provide a good starting place. If the child is not developmentally average, the adult should ignore the "month age" in the titles of the six sections. For example, Nick at twenty months of age can benefit from and enjoy the game "Setting Up for Walking" (in the six-to-twelve-month section). Nick has Down's Syndrome. He and several other special children are lovingly included in the photographs of this book. Their successes and their joy in achievement remind us that we shouldn't be too impressed with the "average" ages given for the activities but should simply use them as they become appropriate for the individual child.

Another aspect of individualization has to do with where you start in the book. It's simplest if your child is a newborn and you move together through the entire set of games. However, if you are the parent of a two-year-old or the teacher of a two-year-old day care group, consider starting before the twenty-four-month section. Many of the earlier games are challenging enough for two's who haven't had the preparation of the entire sequence. Also many games such as "Puzzle Play" have variations that go right on up to developmental age two and even beyond. Be sure not to let the early placement of a game cause you to miss its more advanced variations.

How do I get started?

If you are a parent, you've probably been observing your baby from the start. That is the first step—having a general idea of what your child can do already. For day care professionals who may be just getting to know a baby, this observation period may be a bit more structured.

The checklist at the beginning of each section is a useful tool for identifying a behavior which should be observed before a given Learningame is taught—that is, a child behavior which will be used in the game. You will want to try to notice "new" behaviors or skills as soon as the baby begins to show them. These emerging skills are the ones that are ready to be strengthened easily or used by the Learningames.

How do I match an emerging behavior with the right game?

Once you have noticed an infant behavior or skill that might be used or encouraged in a game, find it in the checklist, make a check by it, and note the number beside it. This number will identify a particular game activity that is probably right for the infant.

You may not always find on the checklist the exact behavior you want to encourage, so look for one that seems similar. Don't expect to make a perfect match of your observation and a Learningame every time. Sometimes you may find that your baby can play a game so well from the start that it bores him. Other times, you may find that a game is still too advanced for him. You can then go back to the table of contents or the checklist or thumb through the neighboring games in the book for a slightly harder or easier game.

How do I play the game?

Remember that for the baby, playing and learning can be the same thing. In playing, he's exercising his curiosity about the world. By helping him satisfy that curiosity and get enjoyment from learning, you are helping to build positive attitudes for that later time when he has much more learning to do on his own.

The first step is to read the game description. Notice that the goal of the game is always a goal for the adult. That is, we reach the goal of the game by doing something with our behavior—not the child's. We hope the child will respond in a particular way, but we can't be sure, and we have no right to insist on it (or any reason to be disappointed if he doesn't).

After you have gathered whatever materials are needed for a particular game, sit down with your baby and enjoy. There is no pressure for the child to do these games in a hurry or to get them exactly "right." First, show him what you are doing (the goal for your behavior, like tapping a pan with a spoon), then let him take over. Give him lots of chances to experiment with the activity.

The experience may last only thirty seconds, or if the baby enjoys the game, he may want to go at it longer than you would prefer. If you begin to tire of it, perhaps you can introduce a new element into the game. But remember, he's enjoying success, and that's one reason he likes to repeat it. If he doesn't catch on to the game right away or gets fussy, give him a little extra help. Or reach a good stopping place and change the game to something you know he can do. It's important to let him get plenty of fun out of your time together; he can always come back some other time to the game that didn't go well.

When and where can I use the games?

The games are varied so that, with a little common sense, some of them can be used just about anytime and anywhere. Some of the language games are good to use when you are diapering the baby or caring for him in some other way. A few of the games the baby can play alone, if you have gotten ready the things he needs. Then, there are other games that require you and the baby to give your full attention to each other; these usually work best when the baby is rested and alert.

Keep in mind that some games require you to have simple materials on hand when you start to play. This takes only the same foresight as making sure you have all the ingredients before you begin to prepare a recipe. The materials are usually in *italic print* on the left-hand page so you can locate them at a glance. Some of the games tell you when they are best used, but most are flexible enough that deciding when and where is really up to you.

Should I stick to the letter of each game, or can I make changes?

The most important part of these Learningames is you. Your observations should be your best guide to choosing games, and to varying them to keep your child's interest. The game description puts you in the ball park, but you call the plays.

Are some ideas the same for all games?

In almost every game you will find yourself doing several basic things: talking, supporting, showing, and varying.

Talking. Even though the baby may not yet understand the meaning of your words, you will want to talk about things with him. Tell him what you are doing. Tell him what he is doing ("You caught the ball!"). Use correct names and grammar. Some of the pages have a special format that illustrates how many language opportunities exist in common situations such as a bath. You will discover similar opportunities throughout the day.

Supporting. Be generous with your smiles, pats, snuggles, and words of encouragement. Don't wait for perfection, start rewarding the child when he just begins to get the hang of the activity, and keep it up until he's got the whole thing. Be especially rewarding when he performs one of the desired behaviors that are described on the left-hand page.

Showing. Because you can't explain an activity to a very young child, you have to show him. Sometimes you demonstrate how to do something new. Sometimes you copy what the baby has just done to "explain" to him that you approve. When he sees you do it, chances are he will do it again.

Varying. If the child's interest in a game begins to lag before he's really mastered the skill, change the game a little. You can also vary a game when **you** start getting bored with it. Adding some variety can make a good game better. It is usually a mistake to play a game only one or two days and then to put it aside. Many repetitions, with slight variations, are much more likely to help your baby. Some of the games have major variations that can stretch out over months or even years of growth.

Do these games have any side effects?

Yes. Both adult and infant learn to work and play as a team and to have fun doing it. The adults sharpen their ability to take note of needs and to contribute to the growth of the child as his teacher. The adults become more aware of the importance of their role in the child's future. And they develop feelings for the child—especially respect—that are deepened by the game interactions. In addition to his new skills, the infant gains confidence in himself and in adults. He learns that people are responsive and helpful and that his actions have a predictable effect on the exciting physical world around him. He continues to build a curiosity and persistence that make him unafraid of approaching new problems.

The adult and child make important contributions to each other: each rewards the other with smiles, communication, and love. And the Learningames are theirs to enjoy together.

0-6 Months

In these early days the infant is able to respond to things that can be seen, heard, and felt and that occur close to her. You will want to be alert to the infant's signals and have ready some appropriate ideas and activities. With this preparation you will have greater opportunities for responding to each moment of infant curiosity.

It may seem odd to think of the activities of the first few months as games. But they are games in the sense that they are carried out in partnership between the adult and child, each responding to the other's move. The caring way in which you observe and answer the infant's expressed needs helps her develop a positive approach to life and trust in you. For at this early age she is entirely dependent on the loving adult for providing the means and encouragement necessary for her to succeed in her attempts at learning about her world. It's a big responsibility, but the essence of what the baby needs is contained in the things you will be doing naturally and comfortably. This, like many other of life's important opportunities, can best be approached with a relaxed attitude.

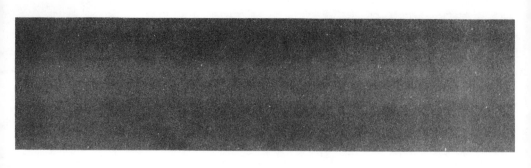
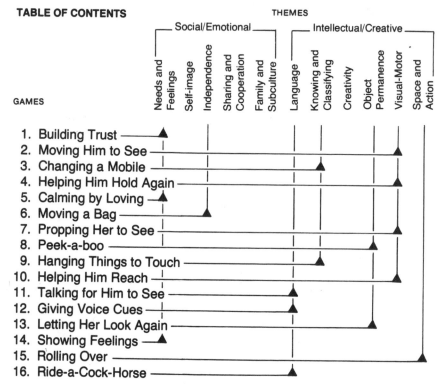
2

Checklist: 0-6 Months
(Developmental Age)

NEW BEHAVIORS	SUGGESTED GAMES	NEW BEHAVIORS	SUGGESTED GAMES
☐ Quiets when picked up	1	☐ Laughs aloud	
☐ Lifts head when held at shoulder	2	☐ Pulls garment over face	8
☐ When on stomach lifts or turns head		☐ Reaches persistently	9
☐ Eyes follow a moving person		☐ Eye-hand coordination in reaching	10
☐ Looks (rather than glances) at suspended object	3	☐ Vocalizes in response to a smile or talking	11
☐ Grasps and holds a person or object for several seconds	4	☐ Knows familiar people or things by sight or voice	
☐ Responds to talking, smiling, or touching		☐ Turns head to sound of bell and rattle	12
☐ Stops crying when someone (without holding) begins to play with him	5	☐ Turns head after a spoon that has fallen from the table	13
☐ Random arm thrusts in play	6	☐ Vocalizes in association with pleasure, displeasure, eagerness, and satisfaction	14
☐ Sits in lap with support	7	☐ Uses vocal noises for play	
☐ Closes hand on dangling toy		☐ Rolls from back to stomach	15
☐ Makes approach movements toward mirror image		☐ Likes frolic play	16
		☐ Cries to get a bottle, attention, or to be held	

3

1. Building Trust

HOW ADULT: Your baby learns to trust and love by feeling the love you express as you hold and care for her. The way in which you respond to her needs, by going quickly to her when she expresses discomfort, shows her you care. □ Hold her close and securely so your own confidence is communicated to her. But don't always wait until she calls. When you feel you'd like to pick her up and love her, do it! It won't "spoil" her. Love is one of her most basic needs just as it's yours. □ Respond to her totally when you're taking care of her needs. Cuddle, rock, talk, and comfort while you're diapering or feeding or bathing. Your words won't have any meaning but your voice and body will tell that you love her and that you treasure her love. □ Feeding can be the most loving time of all. This is a social time for just the two of you. All the things she feels, the taste of the milk, the warmth of your body, the feel of the blanket provide her with tactile experiences. This tiny human is soaking up all these new feelings with her whole body. Think what the baby who's given a propped bottle is missing.

INFANT: The infant's communication is not in spoken words but rather in her watching, snuggling, smiling, and even in her sleeping and lying quietly when she's content. □ Her crying can indicate her confidence in you too—she's learning that her sounds cause something to happen that makes her comfortable again. □ She may begin quite early to coo and smile at the adult and that will earn her even more love. Some babies for a while don't seem to show much response. But the baby is responding in her own way, and the adult must look for these ways and find the patience to go on trusting in the infant's love until those responses become easier to understand.

WHY GOAL: To teach trust while taking care of daily needs. To communicate love in the way you respond.

USES: The baby's trust in one or two important persons is the pattern by which she builds later relationships.

1. Building Trust

HOW Your love for your baby is expressed in the way you pick her up and hold her and talk to her. Give her love when you give her food and fresh diapers. She'll learn from you how to smile and snuggle and coo to give her love back.

WHY To let the baby know it's O.K. to trust you now . . . so she can be ready to trust others in the future

2. Moving Him to See

HOW ADULT: Think about positions that will help the baby effectively use his head and eyes. From the earliest days occasionally hold the baby to your shoulder. Keep your hand near—but let him support his own head as much as he wants. Sit or stand so he sees *something attractive* over your shoulder. (When the baby is less than four months old, he can see things best which are about seven or eight inches from his eyes. This means you need to stand closer than you might expect.) □ Talk to him and stroke him as you hold him. Another person could enter into the game by standing behind you and talking to him. Also think about providing variety in where the baby lies. You can push his crib to the window where he can feel a little breeze or watch the sunlight and shadows moving on the wall. □ As he gets a little older, put him on a blanket indoors or outdoors where you are working so he can see you moving about, and you can see and hear him. As you go about your work, stop and visit with him, stroking him and responding to the sounds he makes.

INFANT: Held at your shoulder, the baby will probably hold his head steady for a moment, then let it drop back. The length of time he can hold it up will get longer and longer. He'll try harder when he sees something interesting that he'd like to see again. □ On his back he may try to turn his head and focus his eyes on nearby things. He is likely to look at the adult, at first following her with his eyes and later turning his head to keep her in view. Sometimes he will look toward her voice and coo and smile, encouraged when she lovingly answers him.

WHY GOAL: To provide interesting positions and situations so he will want to hold his head up and use his eyes.

USES: The baby needs to be able to hold his head steady in order to begin to use the trunk of his body skillfully. The infant's natural curiosity provides him with an interest in discovering new things. We are responsible for encouraging him by holding and placing him in positions that will allow him to use his own body most effectively and by providing many things for him to be curious about.

2. Moving Him to See

HOW Sometimes hold your baby high on your shoulder so he can hold up his own head and look over your shoulder at something pretty. When you put him down to play, be sure there's something interesting and changing to see. Stop by to talk to him and hold him as often as you can.

WHY To show him something interesting so he will want to explore with his eyes

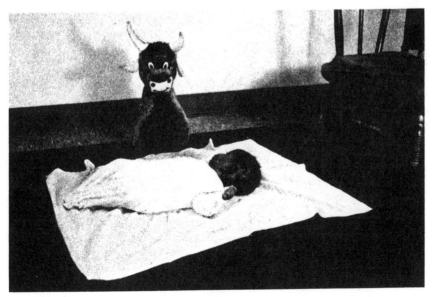

3. Changing a Mobile

HOW ADULT: Almost everyone thinks about having a mobile for a young baby. But usually we put it up and forget about it. The baby can learn much more from a gradually changing mobile than from a static one. This game gives an idea of how to change a homemade mobile. □ Fasten a *dowel* securely across the crib. With a *string* tie a colorful object or a *toy* to the stick so the baby can see it. Talk to him about the toy and jiggle it so he looks at it, then leave the toy there for him to see. In a day or two tie something else beside the first thing and enjoy a few moments calling his attention to it. When he seems to have gotten used to the two things (perhaps several days, perhaps a week), switch the left and right position of the two. After a third thing has been added, take off the first toy. Continue the game by changing one thing every few days. □ If you buy a commercial mobile, you could choose one that may be taken apart. Slowly rearrange or replace the parts so your baby will have the opportunity to notice change in his world.

INFANT: The baby will try to look at the toy and perhaps follow its movement with his eyes. He may move his arms, but probably will not be able to hit it. We expect him to look less at the toys the longer they have been there—because he's "learned" them or become habituated to them. When a change has been made, we expect him to look more at the new toy.

WHY GOAL: To help the baby notice differences by giving him something to look at that changes little by little.

USES: Noticing that the things on the stick are being changed could be a tiny step toward the important ability to notice that one thing is different from another. This ability to tell things apart can continue to develop throughout life and has endless uses. For example, you couldn't read if you couldn't tell one letter from another.

3. Changing a Mobile

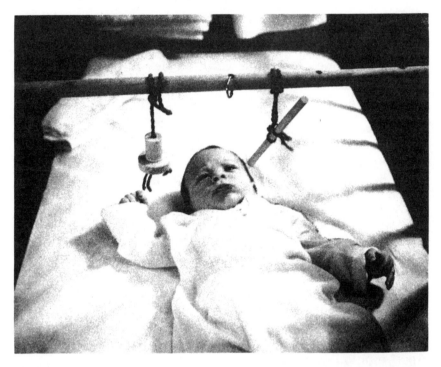

HOW Attach a stick across the crib and hang a colorful toy from it. Enjoy a few minutes jiggling the toy so your baby will be sure to see it. In a few days hang up another toy beside the first. After a third thing has been added, take off the first toy. Keep the game going by changing one thing every week or every few days.

WHY To help the baby begin noticing differences

4. Helping Him Hold Again

HOW ADULT: Hold a *small toy* or a clothespin so the baby can see it. Talk to him about it. Touch the inside of his hand with it to help his fingers close around it. Then take your hand away letting him hold it. When he drops the toy, do it again. Then give him time to rest his hand. Talk pleasantly to him about holding. Touch his hand and enclose it in yours to show him you like what he's doing. ☐ As he gains more control, you may need to fetch the toy more often because he's learning to let go as well as to hold. For a while you may feel you're doing all the work because he will be dropping it more than he's holding it. ☐ Later, vary the game by giving him something that feels quite different, so he'll have more reason for wanting to keep it in his hand. Use things such as a carrot stick or a fuzzy piece of yarn. Give him a chance to use each hand in turn to hold the toy.

INFANT: When he's very little, he holds the toy tightly because he grips on contact and he doesn't yet know how to open his fingers. At this early stage he may hold the toy a long time, perhaps even forgetting it is in his hand. ☐ The real learning starts when he begins to move his fingers more purposefully. Then he is more likely to alternate between holding and dropping the toy. He may hold it for shorter times than he did when he was a few days old, but this is because he's trying out lots of movements with his hands. ☐ As he practices and his fingers get stronger, he'll once again be able to hold on longer, but this time he will be in greater control of his grip.

WHY GOAL: To help the baby practice holding things and to give him various tactile experiences.

USES: Grasping is a start in the lifelong process of learning to use your hands. Consider how many more hand skills there are that follow: pushing a button through, cutting with scissors, etc.

4. Helping Him Hold Again

HOW Hold a small toy for the baby to see. Touch the inside of his hand with it so his fingers close around it. Hand it to him again when he drops it. Speak lovingly to him as you give the toy each time.

WHY To give the baby early practice in using his hands

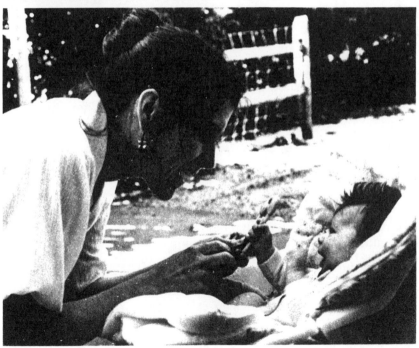

5. Calming by Loving

HOW ADULT: Try to become aware of what helps your baby calm down when she's upset. In the first month the reactions of your infant are said to be reflexive. Her response to her world is very physical. When she's content, she's soft and relaxed all over; but when she's upset, not just her voice but her arms and legs and back as well let you know how unhappy she is. □ To calm her, try responding to her whole body, folding her arms softly against her chest, swaddling her with her *blanket* and holding her close to your warmth. Let her look at you. Then look at her and talk quietly as you hold and stroke her. □ As she gets a little older and is less reflexive in her activity, see if you can begin to calm her sometimes by touching, stroking, and patting as you stand by her crib and talk comfortingly to her. She still needs a lot of holding, so if you can, pick her up after she's been calmed by touching or stroking. □ Later in the first year, your voice, used gently, may sometimes calm her for a minute before you get to her. When she has been comforted and quieted by your voice, make a point of going as soon as you can to stroke her and often to pick her up, to let her see you are there. □ If your baby shows a set of responses different from those described here, observe and learn from her—she's the expert on her needs.

INFANT: In the earliest days the baby needs to be picked up to be calmed. Later she might be calmed for a short time by stroking accompanied by the sound of the voice. When her trust in the adult grows stronger, she will need only to hear comforting words to be soothed until you get there. □ She likes being held, though, and needs it even when she isn't being calmed. Even though we learn about the comfort in a human voice, none of us totally outgrows the need for some physical comforting.

WHY GOAL: To use various ways (holding, stroking, talking) to help the baby feel calm and secure. To adjust your response to her need and reaction.

USES: Learning to trust you will help her to have trust in herself and later in other people. Babies whose cries are responded to promptly in the early months usually cry less later on.

12

5. Calming by Loving

HOW When your baby is upset, she needs your love. To calm her, pick her up and hold her close. Wrap her blanket around her to make her feel secure. Look at her and talk quietly as you cuddle her. When she's older, stroking and talking may calm her sometimes before you pick her up. Notice what works best for your baby.

WHY To get to know your baby so you'll be able to give comfort that is "just right".

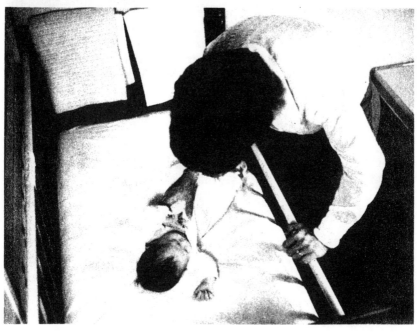

6. Moving a Bag

HOW ADULT: A *bag* on a *string* can provide the infant with a chance to direct her own play as she gains some control over her arm and leg movements. Place the baby on her back in a crib. Tie a flat, colorful paper bag to one end of a piece of thick yarn or an elastic string and tie the other end loosely around one of the infant's wrists. Let the end with the bag hang over the top of the crib side. Tuck the bag back inside to slide along the rails so she can easily see it. As she moves her arms in play, the bag will move. If it doesn't move, the bag may need a small object in it for weight. □ When it moves, pat her tummy and smile at her. When you have responded several times, give her a chance to play alone as you work nearby. You can still show you're interested by talking to her when you see the bag move. □ Change the game on other days by putting the yarn on the other wrist, or try it on her ankle, making sure she's able to see the bag well. Later add something that might make a little noise. □ You know your child well enough to decide when she's through with the game. Untie the bag and pick her up to love her a little as you let her touch the bag.

INFANT: The infant will see the movement first out of the corner of her eye and then by turning her head. When she kicks and wiggles in her play, the bag will shake, and as she continues, she may begin to sort out her movements and be more able to move the bag with her arm only. Hearing the adult's voice after the movement of the bag encourages some babies to try again, but may distract others.

WHY GOAL: To encourage the baby to move her arms (and legs) to make something happen. To let the child control the game.

USES: A child who knows she can make things happen will have a positive approach to new situations. When, for example, she's on her stomach in a new place, she may be more likely to use her arms to reach out to the toys she sees there.

6. Moving a Bag

HOW You can begin early to help your baby do something for herself. Tie a flat, colorful bag to a thick piece of yarn. Gently fasten the other end to her wrist and let the bag hang over the crib. As she waves her arms about, she moves the bag. She will look to see what's happening. She'll enjoy trying to move her arms again to see the movement, and you'll enjoy watching her learn.

WHY To encourage the baby to move her arms and make something happen

> **Safety note:** Of course, nothing should be left tied to the baby unless an adult is in the room and watching.

7. Propping Her to See

HOW ADULT: Place a *squashy pillow* under your baby's chest. This makes it easier for her to hold her head up and look around. Be sure her arms are in front of the pillow. Watch carefully and help her if she slips. ☐ Put some interesting toys in front of her that she can see and play with, or use a mirror so she has "another" baby to watch. Enjoy chatting with her about the things she's looking at and fingering. Take the pillow away and turn her on her back when she seems tired. ☐ As a change from being on her chest or back, set the infant on the floor or in a playpen and prop her with *firm pillows*. Be sure her back is reasonably straight and her arms can move as she balances her own head. Then put a toy in front of her that she can see. ☐ Sometimes put her where she needs to raise her head a little higher so she has a chance to move her head up and down as well as sideways. You may put her in a *cardboard box* with firm pillows inside the box under and in front of her and take her to the room where you are working. Talk to her pleasantly about what you're doing as she watches you. Of course, propping is done only when you're nearby to respond to her needs.

INFANT: At first the infant will not hold her head up very long and will need to rest after a short time. Later she will hold it up longer. On the pillow she may push with her legs or perhaps even roll over sideways. ☐ When she is propped sitting, she can hold her head up for a few minutes, then rest it against her chest or the pillows. She will lift it again to look and reach for the toy or for other things around. She will enjoy being able to see a little farther into the world around her with its changing sights and sounds.

WHY GOAL: To position the baby so she can hold her head up and see more. To help her use her hands more freely when on her stomach or sitting.

USES: When the baby is flat on her stomach, her exploration is limited. Sometimes she seems to see only the rug or the bedsheet. When she is propped, her hands are available to add tactile experiences. As she gains more control over her head movements, she can have a much greater field of exploration.

7. Propping Her to See

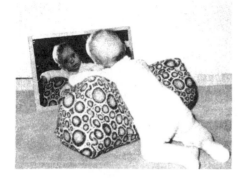

HOW When you want to be with your baby but have something you need to do, take her with you. Put her on her chest on a pillow so her head and arms are free. Give her some things to see and reach for. Or prop her in a box so she can turn her head and look up to see you or look down at some toys. Stopping to talk to her and giving her a pat helps to keep her interested and looking around.

WHY To put the baby in a position that will let her explore more with her eyes and hands

8. Peek-a-boo

HOW ADULT: Lightly cover a part of the baby's face with a *receiving blanket*. Talk to him so he hears your voice as his eyes are covered. Pull the blanket away, saying, "Peek-a-boo!" Be surprised and cuddle him to you when his face appears. Gradually take longer before you pull the blanket down. Sooner or later he may pull it off by himself before you get to it. □ When he successfully pulls it off, let him know how surprised and pleased you are. If he's a little afraid, play gently and be sure he can still see most of the time. If he doesn't like even that, cover your own face and play the game. Wait a few days to see if he's ready to have his face covered. □ You are helping him to understand the permanence of things in his environment, and you want to be sure he enjoys the experience. Have fun playing the game while you are dressing or bathing him. Anything can be used to hide behind: a shirt, a washcloth, a fresh diaper.

INFANT: At first the baby may be suddenly still under the blanket or he may thrash his arms and legs. His first tries to push back the blanket are likely to be little rubbing movements of his fist. He will need a little help in the beginning. As he gets better, he will probably grasp the blanket pulling it off and sometimes trying to pull it up to cover his own face again. □ If you are having fun and show surprise, he smiles and waves his arms and legs as he's uncovered. This is likely to become a favorite game for him to play any time with almost anyone. He may still like this game a year from now.

WHY GOAL: To have fun while the baby begins to learn that you are still there even when he can't see you.

USES: Over a period of many months the child will learn that when people or things go out of sight, they are not necessarily gone forever. But now he doesn't know that, and the "magical" disappearance and reappearance of people makes this game exciting. The permanence of objects and people will become essential to his security as later in exploration he crawls and walks out of sight of familiar areas, he needs to find toys that have been put away, or he does other independent things.

(Like most Learningames, this can be used with developmentally delayed children as seen in bottom photo.)

8. Peek-a-boo

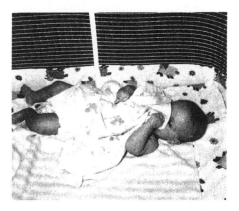

HOW Lightly cover a part of the infant's face with a baby blanket. Talk to him so he hears your voice as his eyes are covered. Pull the blanket away saying, "peek-a-boo!" Be surprised and cuddle him to you because to him it seems that you truly disappeared. Cover your own face sometimes.

WHY To enjoy some time together using a little infant "magic"

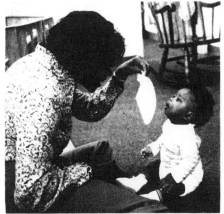

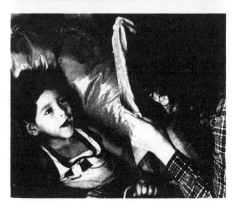

9. Hanging Things to Touch

HOW ADULT: Secure a *dowel* to the crib. Tie on two objects that feel very different, such as a *crocheted square* and a *vegetable brush*. Make the strings long enough for the child to see and touch the feelie objects easily. Laugh and smile while you bring an object to touch his hand; then let it hang while he tries to get it. □ If the baby seems to be paying less attention to his new feel mobile after a few days, take off one of the old objects and add a new one. Everybody likes a change, so you may be able to renew your baby's interest in the mobile every few days by making a small change in it. This game allows the infant to play independently for a few moments before going to sleep or after awaking from a nap. □ Later when the baby has enough control to begin hitting the objects and moving them around, add some sound to his play with *wooden spools* on an *elastic string*. Tie it across the crib low enough for him to touch. Swing or bounce the spools gently so they make a clacking noise. Talk about them so he will notice them. When he has grasped them, he will feel the pull from the elastic and will enjoy the gentle click they make when he releases them. Stop by the crib frequently to smile and talk to him about the sound. □ If you buy a manufactured mobile, look for one that encourages the baby to do something actively.

INFANT: The infant may reach for and swat the objects. He might even have favorites. He may pull his hand away from a stiff or prickly object or make a face. □ When his grasp is better, he will pull them toward his mouth. He will probably look toward any sounds that are made by or near the objects. Like any other person, at times he will be totally disinterested in the mobile!

WHY GOAL: To give the baby many opportunities to reach for things he sees or hears. To let him use several senses together.

USES: He can become familiar with the textures and sounds by using his eye-hand coordination skills. Familiarity with the environment creates the need for further exploration.

9. Hanging Things to Touch

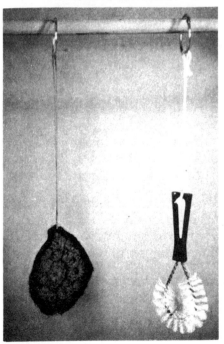

HOW Tie a dowel or a stick across the crib. Attach two things that feel very different. Make the strings long enough for the baby to see and touch the "feelie" things easily. Later, when the baby has enough control to begin hitting the things, add something that will make a sound.

WHY To help the baby feel the things his eyes can see

10. Helping Him Reach

HOW ADULT: Tie a *scarf or necktie* around your neck so the ends dangle in front. Then lean over the baby so he can reach the scarf and clearly see your face. Shake the scarf so he will notice it. At first you can help him by touching the scarf to his hand. Later, just wiggling the scarf and speaking lovingly will encourage him to try to look and reach. □ In this game you are helping him coordinate his eye and hand movements. So when he makes any move toward the scarf, smile and caress him to show you're pleased he's trying. Be sure you put the baby in control by letting him "turn on" your smile when he reaches for or gets the scarf. Your actions will tell him that he is a powerful person who can make things happen—a message we all need to hear! □ This game helps the adult and infant make contact as active partners in a social exchange. Relax and enjoy it. After all, it is a treat to see your baby learning a new skill and reaching out to you.

INFANT: The baby makes only kicking movements and random swatting movements of his hands at first. The good feeling he gets from the adult's smiles and approval encourages him to try again. When he is able to guide his hand better, he may grab on tight, jerking and swinging the scarf. Soon he will probably talk and smile back to this responsive face attached to his "toy." If the adult leads the way, the baby may join in a rollicking good laugh over the whole thing.

WHY GOAL: To help the baby reach and get what he sees. To allow the child to experience a sense of effectiveness and control in a social context.

USES: The infant will need to know how to make his hands and eyes work together to get things for himself. Eye-hand coordination is essential to the exploration of his surroundings now and throughout his life.

10. Helping Him Reach

HOW Tie a scarf around your neck. Lean over the baby so he can reach the scarf and clearly see your face. When he makes any move to touch the scarf, smile and talk to show him he did something special.

WHY To let the baby reach and make something happen

11. Talking for Him to See

HOW ADULT: Hold your baby close with his head cupped in your hands so that he can see your face and lips. Lean toward him and talk happily. Pause expectantly—giving him plenty of time to make his own sounds. When he makes any sound, by accident or intention, smile and talk, repeating his own sound back to him. □ Take your time. You've had lots of time to practice, but vocalizing is new to him, and he may have to really work at it. Your repetition of his sounds and your loving voice and face give him encouragement to try again. □ These "conversations" with the child can begin at an early age, but they are so much fun and can teach so much that they should be a frequent game at every age. Of course, you and the child will discover new sounds to make back and forth with your voices as he gains new skills. □ As he gets older, you won't need to hold his head and he can sit in any comfortable position facing you on your lap.

INFANT: The baby will watch your face and lips if you move them so he can see clearly. (At this early age things that are about seven or eight inches away are in clearest focus for him.) He may smile because he likes to have the adult talk to him, but he may not try to make sounds right at first. When he's ready, he will begin. □ His sounds will, of course, not be like the adult's, but they may seem to be in answer to her. He has to get a lot of things together—the sound of the adult's voice, the sight of her lips moving, and the effort of making his own voice and mouth work. His whole body will work at it as he tries. □ These times of close sharing are enjoyable to him if the adult is relaxed and enjoying them too.

WHY GOAL: To help the baby know that sounds and mouth movement usually go together, and to encourage him to watch your face as you talk. To allow him to experience the pleasure of back-and-forth vocalization.

USES: The baby will need to practice making mouth noises so he can later learn to talk. We believe that later the infant will imitate the mouth movements he has seen as well as the mouth sounds he has heard.

11. Talking for Him to See

HOW Hold your baby close so he can see your face and lips. Talk happily to him. Then pause and listen for him to make baby sounds. If he does, repeat his sounds. Let your face and voice show him you like it when he makes a sound . . . because these little sounds are the bits and pieces from which he will later make words.

WHY To help the baby know that sounds and mouth movements go together

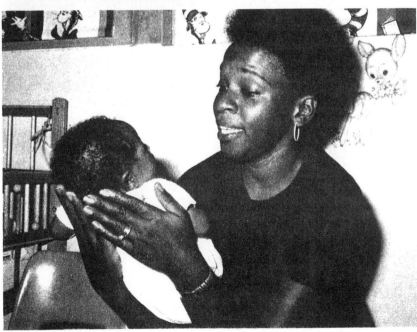

12. Giving Voice Cues

HOW ADULT: When the infant is on her back on the floor, move to a position four or five feet to the side of her head without letting her see you. Stoop and speak her name softly several times. If she makes no attempt to turn toward your voice, repeat her name a little louder. If she makes tentative movements but doesn't turn enough to see you, call again to help her. ☐ When she turns her head toward your voice enough to see you, laugh, pick her up, and cuddle her for a minute. Again lay her down and repeat the calling game from her other side. You are helping her to explore with her ears so you will want to try to stay out of her sight until she has turned her head enough to make eye contact. You are the object she was searching for, so be sure to allow her to have her reward—you. ☐ Another time play the game with the infant on her stomach. As she gets more control and can turn her head a little more quickly, praise her a moment with your voice before you go to hug her.

INFANT: The infant may first respond by searching with her eyes. This has been a successful way to discover things so far in her life, but now if the adult is not close enough to be seen, she will probably try a new method—turning her head. ☐ Her first movements may be very slight. The loving voice will encourage her because it's a part of something that makes her happy. When she's on her back, it will be a little easier for her to turn to the voice. On her stomach she has to manage the weight of her head as well as the direction, so she may not look as quickly or for as long. ☐ She enjoys this game throughout the day: when the adult calls quietly from the door as she wakes from her nap or from across the room as he comes to feed her. ☐ If given time, the infant will turn her head and perhaps give her best reward to the adult—a big smile.

WHY GOAL: To make some distant sounds that the infant can search for. To help her use hearing for learning.

USES: By locating sounds whose source is out of sight the infant can begin to extend her field of exploration. As she grows older, she will learn from sounds such as a voice from another room, recorded music, or signals for safety.

12. Giving Voice Cues

HOW Lovingly speak your baby's name as you go to her and she may have a smile ready when you get there. Help her to hear you speak from a distance by calling her name softly before she sees you. Stand still and give her time to turn her head toward your voice. When she's turned enough to look at you, go to her and cuddle her up in your arms.

WHY To make some sounds that will help your baby become alert to language

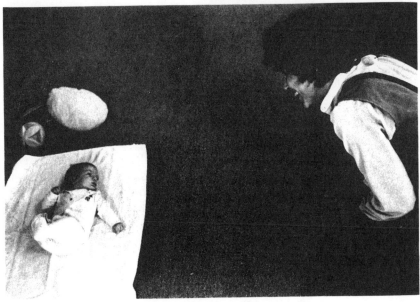

13. Letting Her Look Again

HOW ADULT: The adult sits before a table with the infant on his lap facing the table. He shows her a *favorite toy* and places it on the table, talking about it briefly. He then turns the infant away so her back is to the object. □ If the baby tries at all to turn her head or body and see the object, the adult encourages and helps her. He lets her have the toy, talking to her about finding it and adding smiles and hugs to his words. If the baby doesn't seem to have any memory of seeing it and makes no effort to turn, the adult tries again at a later time. □ To play the game a different way, place the child on the floor on her stomach with the toy in front of her and give her a chance to see it. Slide her quickly around so the toy is at her side (from twelve-o'clock to three-o'clock position). She may wiggle or "crawl" back to the original position or turn herself onto her back in her search. □ If she makes any effort, help her and reward her by giving her the toy. You are trying to help her remember, so watch her carefully; and if you can tell she's trying to find it again, give her time to try for herself. Help her if she needs it.

INFANT: The child may show she is interested in the toy by her facial expression or by reaching for it. When she is turned away, she may try turning first her head and then her body to see it again. When she has turned, she may show she is pleased at having "found" the toy again and will want it to play with. She'll know from the hugs that she did a good thing. □ If she shows no interest at all after it's out of sight, she's not ready for the game. Play something else with her and try this game another time.

WHY GOAL: To help her begin to remember what she sees. To help her bring an object back into sight.

USES: When she remembers things, she will not have to learn the same thing over and over. Memory develops in stages, just as do all her other skills. And turning her head or body to regain sight of something shows she is now starting to develop the type of memory called object permanence.

13. Letting Her Look Again

HOW Help your baby begin to remember things. Show her a toy, then turn her away so it's out of her sight. If she turns back to find it, let her have it to play with. Hug her as you give it to her to show you're pleased she turned to look at it.

WHY To help her begin to remember what she has just seen

14. Showing Feelings

HOW ADULT: Hold the baby around her chest and under her arms. Raise her over your head gently and slowly saying, "Up" or "Up you go." Lower her saying, "Down you come," then cuddle her close. Smile, laugh, and talk so she can tell by your face and words that you, too, have happy feelings about the game and that her feeling of excitement is appropriate. □ Go slowly and give her time to smile and "talk" back to you. You won't want to startle her with movement that is too fast. Maintaining eye contact is a good way to keep her from feeling separated or lost in space. You have the opportunity to fill the day with shared good feelings as you lift her in and out of her crib, onto the changing table, or down to play on her blanket!

INFANT: The child may look a little startled or gasp a little when she's lifted high if this is new to her. When she sees the adult smiling, she will begin to feel good about the movement. She may smile back or chuckle aloud because that's how she sees the adult showing pleasure in the game. Over a period of time she will also begin to understand that "up" and "down" tell her what's happening to her body.

WHY GOAL: To express your excitement and happiness freely so the infant will be encouraged to join in the expression of these same feelings. To use words that tell her what's happening.

USES: Expressing several basic emotions is not difficult for an infant, but she can learn which emotions are appropriate for which occasions from the adults around her. Having seen loved adults showing a joyful approach to games and learning, the child will be more likely to have this same positive approach.

14. Showing Feelings

HOW Hold the baby around her chest. Gently raise her over your head, saying "up." Lower her, saying "down," and cuddle her close. While playing this game, let your face and voice tell her you're happy and excited so she will be encouraged to show she's happy, too.

WHY To express how you are feeling so your baby will know that her feelings are O.K.

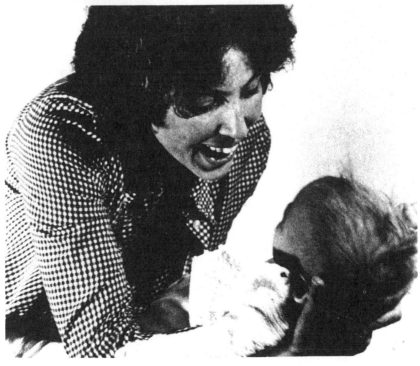

15. Rolling Over

HOW ADULT: The adult places the diapered child on his back on a *smooth surface*. Next to him she places a *fuzzy or textured cloth* onto which he can roll. Sitting or kneeling behind his head, she holds a small attractive object over the child so he can see it comfortably. An *object or toy* that makes a sound will work well. She moves the object gradually to the side and toward the top of the child's head so he must turn his head to keep it in view, saying, "Here it is. It's going." She moves the object slowly and gives him time to follow it with his eyes. ☐ If the child reaches, begins to arch his back and turn his head, she encourages him with words, but does not help him with her hands. When he turns over, she lets him have the object to play with. If things are going well, she repeats from the other side. ☐ If after several tries he turns his upper body but doesn't follow with his legs, she can put her hand on his bottom and gently push to help him get the feel of rolling over. If he doesn't try at all she goes on to something else he enjoys and saves this game till he's ready. When he knows how to roll, surprise him sometimes with a noise maker he can find on his own.

INFANT: The infant will follow the object with his eyes at first. Later he may turn his head and make some attempt to roll his body in his efforts to keep the object in sight. When it is moved toward the top of his head, he may turn first his upper body in his efforts to see. Usually his lower body follows. When he rolls onto the fuzzy surface, he may notice the texture and rub it with his hands.

WHY GOAL: To encourage the child to turn from his back to his stomach. To make turning a rewarding experience by giving the child a new toy, a new texture, a new viewpoint.

USES: He will need to know how to turn over to be able to crawl, change position, and make himself comfortable. Consciousness of the body as a whole leads to the intentional movements of crawling and walking, which make the physical world available for exploration.

15. Rolling Over

HOW When the baby's lying on his back, sit behind his head and hold a little toy above his face. Slowly move it away toward the side and the top of his head, making sure he keeps looking at it. When he turns over trying to see or reach, give him a big hug and let him have the toy. (If he doesn't try, save the game for later.)

WHY To encourage the child to turn over and explore

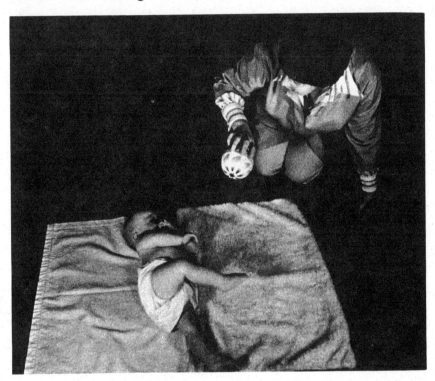

16. Ride-a-Cock-Horse

HOW Adult: Hold your baby on your lap and gently bounce her. Sing a song such as "Ride-a-Cock-Horse" and move her to the rhythm of the song. As you say "goes," bounce her higher. Start slowly. Watch her face and let her see yours so you can read each other's feelings. □ When she's a little older, she can ride on your foot. Swing your leg to the time of the singing and kick a little higher when you say "goes." If you always bounce her higher on the same word, she will begin to expect it. Watch her so you'll know her unique way of telling you she's getting ready. Perhaps you'll find another song that becomes a family favorite for the game.

> Ride a cock-horse, to Banbury Cross,
> To see a fine lady upon a white horse;
> Rings on her fingers, and bells on her toes,
> She shall have music wherever she GOES.

Infant: Babies enjoy all kinds of rhythm games when they're played with an adult they trust. As the child plays this game, she begins to expect the big bounce when she hears "goes" because she's had the simultaneous clues of the word and of the movement of her body. If the game has been gently played, she will not startle. She may coo and chuckle in response to the fun. This may be a favorite game even until the time she can sing some of the words with you.

WHY Goal: To help the baby feel rhythm in language and look forward to a special word, which signals a special event.

Uses: The child needs to know that words can tell her what is happening to her. Hearing a rhyme repeated in the same pleasant circumstances gives her confidence in her own ability to anticipate.

16. Ride-a-Cock-Horse

HOW Sing a nursery song to your baby. Bounce her gently to the time of the music. Bounce her a little higher when you say one particular word. When you repeat it always give the big bounce on the same word. Be prepared for laughs and chuckles from her. Join her in them.

WHY To help the baby look forward to a special word and a special action

6-12 Months

Deliberate actions become the infant's style now as he begins to move about more on his own by rolling, crawling, and pulling up. His improved eye-hand coordination make it possible for him to obtain and explore more things with his mouth as well as his fingers—although his interest in each object may be only momentary.

Watch how he uses his hands, then repeat the motion more deliberately. In doing this you're teaching him to use imitation and repetition, two powerful learning tools.

Listen for the sounds he makes and imitate them so he will get the idea of repeating them. Sometimes you'll hear him practicing by repeating sounds over and over to himself, da-da-da-da, as he plays.

Respond to his interest in language by reading and talking to him. Books with large, single-object pictures of familiar things are good. At other times he's happy just listening to the sound of words as you and other people use them.

The many new and "cute" things he does at this period make it tempting to begin comparing his behavior with that of other infants. But the wise parent will continue to enjoy him as a unique infant and will lovingly encourage his new skills whenever they emerge.

TABLE OF CONTENTS

Checklist: 6-12 Months
(Developmental Age)

NEW BEHAVIORS	SUGGESTED GAMES
☐ Sits alone, steadily	17
☐ Playful response to mirror image (laughing, patting)	18
☐ Has method of getting from one place to another	
☐ Drinks from a cup with some help	
☐ Uses thumb and forefinger to pick up small things	
☐ Uncovers toy purposefully	19
☐ Looks at specific picture in book	20
☐ Says "da-da" or equivalent	21
☐ Shows likes or dislikes of some people, objects, or places	
☐ Looks for something that has been put in a box	22
☐ Drops small object into larger container	23
☐ Imitates actions (such as stirring with spoon in cup)	24
☐ Walks with help	25
☐ Understands "no"	
☐ Regards new person briefly with show of interest or response	26

NEW BEHAVIORS	SUGGESTED GAMES
☐ Attempts some recognizable imitation of words	27
☐ Anticipates sequence of some familiar events	28
☐ Sometimes comes when he is called	
☐ Repeats action that is socially reinforced	29
☐ Uses motions as a way of talking (shakes head "no"; holds out arms to be picked up)	
☐ Attends and responds to adult actions and words across room	30
☐ Demonstrates food preference	31
☐ Searches in the right place for a thing that has been moved out of his sight	32
☐ Knows what some familiar things are for	33
☐ Uses crayons with definite attempts to make marks	34

39

17. Making It Fun to Sit Tall

HOW ADULT: The age when your baby sits alone depends on his own timing. But when he's trying, you can aid by creating a situation for him that will make him want to look up and reach high. This will help to strengthen his back so he can sit for longer periods unpropped. □ Hang a *toy* very securely from a table or chair at the level of his face and shoulders. (When the baby pulls, it must be able to support the pull.) Put a big *pillow* by it and then seat the child on the floor, propped comfortably and in such a position that he can see and reach the toy. Draw his attention to it and let him play. □ Watch to see that he is interested and comfortable. When passing, talk to him about the toy and what he is doing with it. "You're reaching high," or "That's a pretty noise." Sit down beside him and play for a minute. When he rolls over, let him rest or set him up again if he's ready. □ Hanging toys in several places around the house makes it easy for you to take him along and enjoy his company as you do your own thing and it gives him variety to keep him interested.

CHILD: Most of the time the baby will sit in a slumped position. When his attention is drawn to the toy, the child may hold his head up, making his back momentarily straighter. He'll probably try to hit at the toy when he sees it. He may grab and not know how to let go, so he's supporting his weight by holding on to the toy. □ As he plays longer, he will learn to release the toy and still hold himself in a more upright posture for a few seconds. He may roll back onto the pillows when he unbalances. This won't upset him if the adult comes to help him see that it's all part of the fun. He'll enjoy a rest from sitting if he's put on his back after a while with something new to look at.

WHY GOAL: To encourage the child to stretch and balance himself when he is learning to sit alone. To provide something interesting to do while he's sitting.

USES: Sitting alone allows him to use his hands for manipulating the things rather than for supporting his own body. Seeing more distant things will eventually inspire him to try new ways, such as crawling, to get them.

17. Making It Fun to Sit Tall

HOW Toys hanging high will encourage your baby to look up and reach up. This helps him sit alone better. Put a pillow behind him for the times he tumbles. Keep him in sight and let him hear your voice. Show him you're interested by going to hold him and to talk happily with him sometimes about his play.

WHY To encourage the child to explore with his hands from a sitting position

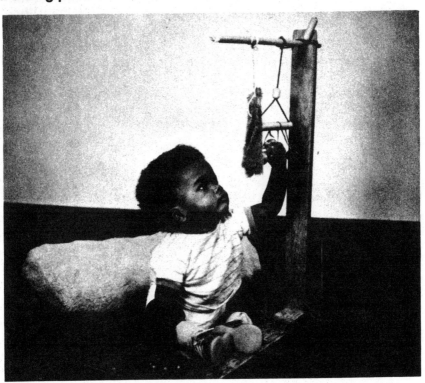

18. Naming with a Mirror

HOW ADULT: The adult holds the child in his arms before a *mirror*. He says something like "See the baby?" or "See Annie in the mirror?" He touches the child's mouth and says, "Mouth; this is Annie's mouth." After several days of playing this game, the adult only says the word, "mouth" or asks the question, "Where is your mouth?" and lets the child try to touch her own mouth. □ He gently helps if she touches the wrong part or doesn't try at all. The adult repeats, touching other parts of the baby's body. If the adult also responds to the many surprising things the baby discovers, this is indeed a pleasant experience for both of them and can be an ongoing game that each time repeats something familiar but adds something new.

CHILD: Feeling the touch of the adult's finger on her mouth at the same time she sees the mouth in the mirror being touched gives her a double clue to the word. She may show some surprise at seeing the adult in two places and look back and forth from the familiar face beside her to the image in the mirror. □ For some time she will think of her image as another baby, but the touching helps her slowly understand. She may try to touch the eye of the image but will find it difficult because the image will move, of course, as she does. Some babies try to look around behind the mirror to see how it works.

WHY GOAL: To start the child on the way to knowing that the mirror gives an image of herself and so to broaden her self-concept. To help her recognize words for body parts.

USES: Think how useful it is for your child to understand words for body parts when you say during a normal day, "Time to wash your face," "Guess what's in my hand," etc. A growing understanding and knowledge of her body as an object in space contributes to the infant's trust in herself as she explores. A positive self-concept, we believe, is important because it can help her approach the world with confidence throughout her life. This and other games provide a small start on that confidence.

18. Naming with a Mirror

HOW Place a mirror where the child can easily see herself. Touch the child's mouth and say, "mouth." Smile to show your own delight as she looks at the baby in the mirror. Help her to touch her own nose. Soon she'll begin to know herself.

WHY To let the child know that she can learn about herself in the mirror

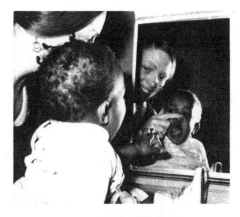

19. Peek-a-boo Mirror

HOW ADULT: Attach a *cloth* to the top edge of a *mirror* that is sturdy and securely mounted. Hold the baby on your lap in front of the uncovered mirror. Point to the image and talk about the baby, then cover the mirror. Ask, "Where is Joan?" and raise the cloth to let her see herself. Be delighted to see the baby again as you say, "There she is!" Repeat, saying what seems comfortable to you, such as "Peek-a-boo" or "Where's the baby?" □ As soon as she begins to understand the game, encourage her to lift the cloth. When she does, be sure to point out that she did it. And continue to show your enjoyment of the game. (If it's convenient, a mirror can be mounted low on a wall with a cloth fastened securely at the top of it. The baby can be set in front of it or allowed to crawl to it to play by herself while you watch from a discreet distance.)

CHILD: When the adult first pulls the cloth back, the baby may be very surprised to see her image. She will soon want to pull the cloth itself, and may uncover the mirror by accident. Then she may pat and talk to the image which she thinks is another baby. She may look back at the adult to try to understand how the adult can be in the mirror and holding her at the same time.

WHY GOAL: To help her learn that she can find her image any time she tries to. To broaden her understanding of herself as a person.

USES: As the baby grows older, she will often need to find things when they are "lost." She will also need to think about people who have gone out of sight.

19. Peek-a-boo Mirror

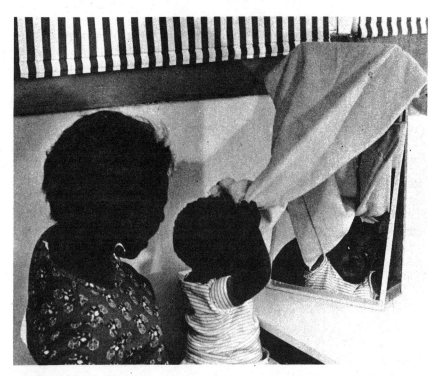

HOW With the baby on your lap sit in front of a mirror. Talk about the baby you see there. Drop a cloth over the mirror, "Where is Joan?" Lift the cloth and say, "There she is!" Drop the cloth again and see if she will search for the mirror image. Be surprised with her when she finds the baby. Be sure to tell her she did it.

WHY To help the child learn that she can be the one to find her image

20. Reading Pictures and Books

HOW Adult: Show a *card* to the child and name the *picture* on it. Tell her in simple words about its color, shape, or use. (Each card should have one specific label to identify it—such as "shoe.") Give her the card to hold, saying "shoe." When the baby shows it back to you, again repeat the name. □ Allow her to keep the card with her toys and play with it. In another day or so give her a new one. Later it's an easy step from using several cards together to using a simple *book of objects* familiar to the child. □ Hold her and show her a picture in the book. Again talk in simple language about the object. Say, "That's a cat," "The cat is furry," "You have a toy cat." Sometimes when you're getting her book, find her toy cat; and as you look at the picture, let her handle the toy. Put it beside the picture so she can see them together. Invite her to say "cat." When she makes a sound be pleased and tell her, "You said cat," or "You're talking." □ Don't expect her to say the word correctly. Just hug her to show you're happy she tried and happy she's having fun with words and pictures.

Child: The child may look at the card, feel it, point to the picture, or put her mouth to it. At first she will learn from the way the adult treats it that this is a different kind of toy. She will soon understand the special fun of listening. She's likely to pick a favorite card and later a book and want to see it over and over. Much of her enjoyment comes from having this special time when she has the adult's loving attention all to herself.

WHY Goal: To show the baby that pictures represent real things and that things and pictures have names.

Uses: Pictures and books are important learning resources that are used throughout life. A positive introduction to them is an important gift from parent to child.

20. Reading Pictures and Books

HOW Enjoy a very personal time with your baby, showing her pictures. Soon you can read simple picture books together. You'll both begin to treasure these times that belong just to the two of you.

WHY To show the baby that things and pictures have names . . . and to build a happy feeling about books

21. Making La-La-La Sounds

HOW ADULT: Watch for the exciting time when the baby, on her own, begins to repeat some sound over and over (lalling). When this happens, hold the child so your faces are close and repeat the baby's sound or another, such as "la-la-la-la." Move your lips slowly and distinctly, making the sound very clear. Watch carefully for signs that the infant is trying to repeat, and encourage her by allowing her plenty of time and by giving the cue again and again if it's needed. □ When the child makes just random sounds, acknowledge them ("You're talking") but continue gently to repeat the particular sound ("Now, say la-la-la"). Encourage only one sound at a time. □ Some sounds that you might expect to pick up from the child are da, ma, bi, and me. Making the sound into a little song by changing your voice pitch or the tempo of the syllables keeps the baby interested and trying longer.

CHILD: The child will learn a sound much more quickly after she has made it once accidentally. By now the baby can focus on objects at any distance, but being close to the adult's face helps her concentrate on the movement of the mouth. She will begin to move her own lips and tongue and produce some sounds. □ After enough tries, she will be able to imitate the particular sound she hears from the adult. This may not happen on the first or even the tenth day they play this game together, but in each session she's gaining more control.

WHY GOAL: To make repeated syllable or wordlike sounds that will encourage the child's lalling.

USES: It's nice for the child to make a sound once. But, when she repeats it over and over, she is well on the way to being able to call that sound back at a later time and to distinguish it from others.

21. Making La-La-La Sounds

HOW Hold the baby so she can see your face. Repeat a sound you have heard her say, such as la-la-la or da-da-da. Give her time to say it back. Let your face show your pleasure when she says the same sound back. If she doesn't seem ready to repeat, simply enjoy the time being together.

WHY To make repeated wordlike sounds that the baby might copy

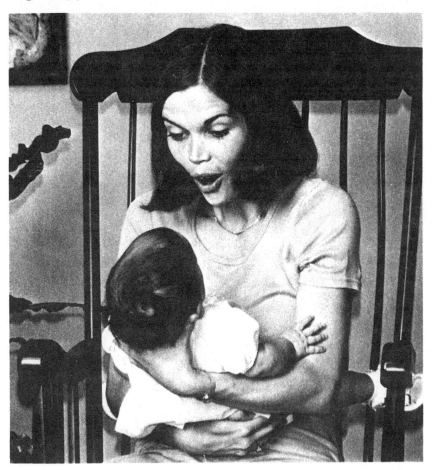

22. Hiding and Finding

HOW ADULT: While you're playing on the floor with the baby, show her a *special toy*. Talk about it and let her handle it while you keep it in your hand. Then let her see you hide it behind you and say, "Where did the doggie go?" "Where is it?" "Can you see it?" □ If the baby doesn't look for it, show it to her again, and then hide it so that a part of it can still be seen. If she looks toward it, tell her, "Great! You found it—you saw it," and bring it out for her to play. Or she may get it for herself by crawling around you. □ Next time hide it in another place—perhaps in your *pocket*. Then she can see the bulge and have fun digging into the pocket for it. Exaggerate a little, to let her know she did a really great thing when she looked for it. Clap and laugh and really enjoy her success. As you dress her or rock her or care for her throughout the day, find ways to hide something that she can find.

CHILD: The child will be interested in the toy but may not the first few times try to look for it when it's hidden. With the youngest babies, "out of sight is out of mind," so your baby may not be ready yet to play. □ When she begins to play, she'll look at the place where it was, reach for it, or crawl around to get it. She'll really be pleased to find it and perhaps will show in her own way that she wants to play again. □ The game becomes more important than the toy. She might laugh and look at her partner to share her pleasure at finding it again. Once in a while the baby will find her own way to "hide" the toy by clutching it to her chest and bending over it. If she isn't looking at it, she probably thinks no one else can see it either.

WHY GOAL: To let the child see an object being hidden. To help the child understand that things she no longer sees can still be someplace else.

USES: Knowing that things she sees hidden still exist (even though she no longer sees them) is a step toward understanding object permanence. As the child's world grows in size and complexity, confidence in that world depends on the stability created by the understanding of the permanence of things and people.

22. Hiding and Finding

HOW When you're having a play time with your baby, show her a special toy. Tuck it in your pocket with a little bit showing. See if she will look for it. Ask, "Where is it?" Let her play with it a minute after you've given her a big hug for finding it. Play again by hiding the toy behind you.

WHY To help the child look for things she sees hidden

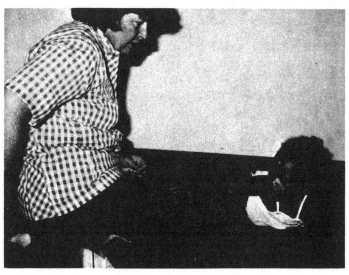

23. Helping Her Let Go

HOW ADULT: You helped your baby to hold on to things when she was quite little. Now she can hold things very well but can't always let them go when she wants because that takes a different set of muscles, and her fingers don't always do what she wants them to. Invent some games that enable her to open her fingers to make something happen. Show her a toy in your hand and when she's looking spread your fingers wide and let the toy drop. Do it again saying "drop" as you open your hand. Use a *ball* that bounces or a *bell* that makes a noise when it hits. Or drop a solid object on to something that will create a sound—such as a *spoon* on a *pan lid*. ☐ Keep a short dropping distance so she'll be able to see your hand and the dropped object at the same time. After you've shown her several times, give her the toy and let her try. This may be really hard for her to do at first, so don't be discouraged if you play a number of days before she begins. Because it is difficult, she'll need your most enthusiastic praise each time she manages to do it. You'll find lots of times to play, such as bath time, when she can make splashes as she drops the soap.

CHILD: First the child may want to just play with the toy. Even when she begins to try, she will hold on to the toy and tap the table top with it or lay it on the table. Her fingers will move a little on the toy in her efforts. She may not even be interested unless something funny happens when the toy is dropped. She doesn't know she's learning to control her fingers—she's trying to make the noise. Seeing the widely spread fingers of her partner will help give her the idea, as will the word "drop." After she's learned how, she'll want to continue the game. Listen to hear if she says something that sounds a little like "drop" as she lets go.

WHY GOAL: To give her practice in hand control by letting go of things. To teach her what the word "drop" means.

USES: Opening the fingers is a different process from closing them, and control of the movement is a learned skill. Early hand control permits the beginning of independence in feeding and broadens the possibilities for exploration by more effective manipulation of the objects in the child's environment. The reason a very young child can't stack blocks well is that she usually can't let go at the exact moment she wants to.

23. Helping Her Let Go

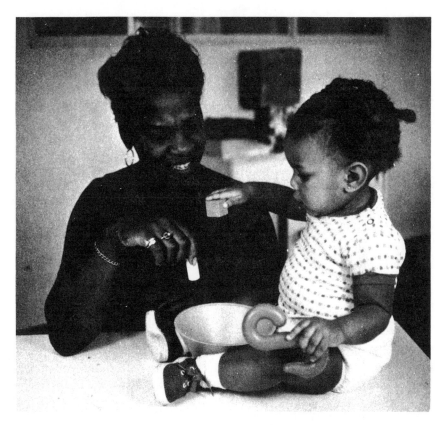

HOW Show your baby a bell or small toy that will make a noise. Turn your hand over, spread your fingers wide, and drop the bell. She'll like the noise and want to try it. Do the same thing with a small ball that bounces when she drops it. She's learning how to make her fingers do what she wants, and you'll enjoy finding new ways to let her try.

WHY To give her practice that will help her gradually gain hand control

24. Imitating Actions

HOW ADULT: The adult and child sit together. The adult holds a *spoon* and a *pan* and gives the child a second spoon. She then hits the pan with the spoon, saying something like "Bang, bang, bang." She repeats this several times and invites the child to join in. When he does, the adult praises him—for example, "You made a good bang," "You did what I did," "I like playing this game with you." □ Imitation depends on how well the child observes and whether he has the skills for the particular action. The adult helps by choosing simple, exciting movements and by repeating and exaggerating her own movements if necessary. Songs and rhymes such as "Pat-a-cake" make the games even more fun and give the child clear, repeated words to hear. □ At first, imitation is taught by taking time out to sit down and show a particular behavior. Later, imitation games can be played "on the wing." That is, the adult doesn't have to completely stop what she's doing—she can just pause for thirty seconds and do something she thinks the child can imitate. □ Some things that take only a moment are:

DO 1.	clap hands once	**SAY**	"clap"
2.	make kissing sounds		"kiss"
3.	spread arms wide		"big"

CHILD: The child is a natural imitator, but his own personality will determine his response to the adult. If he's an active baby, he might jump right in and start banging with a spoon. If he likes to approach things more cautiously, he may spend quite a time observing before he's ready to begin. □ At first his movements may be incomplete. The adult's approval shows him he's on the right track, so he'll keep trying and improving. And when the adult copies him, it makes him feel really good about what he's done.

WHY GOAL: To give the child some actions to imitate. To help the child learn to do a variety of things through enjoyable practice in imitating.

USES: Imitation is a skill acquired early by most children. Sharpening this skill through intentional activities and practice enhances the child's potential for learning many other skills, such as eating with a fork, talking, or riding a bike—all of which are dependent to some degree upon good imitation.

24. Imitating Actions

HOW Doing what he sees you do pleases your baby. Help him to learn by showing him how to copy you better. Bang with your spoon on a pan. Ask him to bang with his spoon just as you did. Tell him, "You did just what I did." Sometimes encourage him to copy you when you clap your hands or spread your arms or throw a kiss. Think up other copying games you can have fun with together.

WHY To help the child use imitation as a frequent way of learning

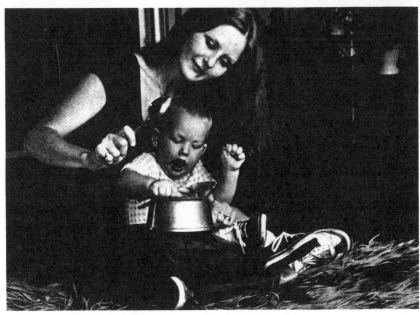

25. Setting Up for Walking

HOW ADULT: For the child who's pulling up to support himself, the adult can set up the environment to encourage walking. For example, the adult places some *chairs* in a row. She puts a *toy* on the first chair and stands the child in front of it. When he's played with the toy for a minute she places a new toy on the next chair making sure the child notices it. Standing behind or beside the chairs, she encourages him to move from chair to chair. (At first it's better to have the chairs almost touching, but as the child becomes more skillful, they are gradually moved apart until he needs to take a free step to get from one to the other.) □ When he's tired of the game, she picks him up and cuddles him a little before giving him a toy on the floor. Later, the adult lets the baby move independently about the room with the support of a *cardboard box*. (This won't work on a rug.) The adult carefully stands the child beside the box, placing his hands on one edge and supporting him until he gets his balance. The box is more resistant than something with wheels and will not run away with the baby. When he pushes it into something, neither he nor the furniture gets hurt.

CHILD: The child leans against the chair to support himself. When he's more sure of himself, he'll depend less on the support of the chairs, but he'll like having them there to grab when he needs to. He may get very interested in one toy and slide down to the floor and play with it. That's okay; there's no hurry about walking. □ When he's walking with the box, he may move it accidently at first as he shuffles his feet to maintain his balance, or if there's a toy on the other end, his efforts to reach it may cause him to walk, like the donkey with the carrot. □ Most babies seem to be as aware as the adults that walking is a very special accomplishment. Their smiles show how "big" they feel.

WHY GOAL: To help the child support his own weight and determine his own balance as he practices walking.

USES: Walking makes available a fascinating new world of physical space.

25. Setting Up for Walking

HOW It's hard to tell who's most proud when your baby first walks—you or the baby. Make it easier for him to walk by giving him things to hold to. Set up some chairs so he can move from one to the other. [Put a toy on each chair so he will want to move to it.] Give him a box to push, or let him hold on to one end of a stick.

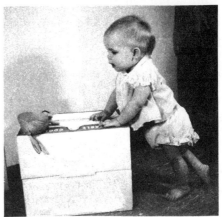

WHY To arrange things that will help him walk independently

26. Introducing Strangers

HOW Adult: Hold your baby in the security of your arms when she is meeting a new person. Look toward the person as you say his name and extend your hand to him. If she seems willing, help her touch the other's hand for a minute. Most babies between six and twelve months prefer familiar persons, and it is appropriate for her to be a little distant with visitors, even aunts and grandparents. □ Give them a different way to become acquainted. Let the visitor hand the child her *toy* or show her something pretty like a *flower*. Another time you can give the baby something to show or hand to the visitor. □ When she is ready to go to the adult at this or a later visit, stay close so she can see you, but don't try to maintain eye contact. Things may work better if you appear to be busy with something else nearby. You can be ready to hold her again when she indicates she's had enough of this new experience.

Child: Earlier the child would go to almost any adult. Now she will often prefer to get to know another adult by watching him first from the security of familiar arms. Fondling a toy extended to her by the new adult is like getting to know a part of the person, and she is often willing to do that. □ When she makes her first visit to the lap of the other adult, it may be for only a second and she's ready to go "home" to mother or daddy. Later she'll stay long enough to look and touch and learn about this new person.

WHY Goal: To pave the way for the child to feel comfortable with new people.

Uses: The child is curious about new things in her environment, including people. Now she is expressing her preference for a few special adults, but confidence will give her a widening circle of contacts that will enrich her experience.

26. Introducing Strangers

HOW Hold your baby in your arms when she meets new people. Let her watch and listen to get to know them. Help other people to respect her feelings and approach her gently. The new friend can "make contact" at first by handing her something. Let her decide when she's ready for them to hold her. Stay close when she is held so she has the comfort of an old friend sharing this experience with her.

WHY To help the child feel comfortable with new people

27. "Hi" and "Bye-bye"

HOW ADULT: After you hear your child using the sound "ah" or a sound like it, repeat "hi," smiling and gesturing while saying it. Do this either when approaching the child or when the child makes a sound resembling "ah" or "hi." It's not always necessary to use your hand but since it helps the baby to notice, use it whenever you can. □ If you are changing diapers or have your hands full and the child makes the sound, put your face close and, smiling, repeat "hi," but go on with what you are doing. When he finally does say "hi" and raises his hand, your delight will make him smile even more. And there may be real reason for delight, because this is probably his first conversation with real words. □ Saying "bye-bye" to the baby when you leave the room helps to prepare him for the exit. Wave your hand near your face as you say it to help him see that both hand and mouth have something to do. Sometimes help him wiggle his fingers while you say "bye-bye." Have other people, especially siblings, wave to him; or stand outside the house and let him wave to passers-by—most will happily wave back.

CHILD: The child will listen and watch—at first smiling back at the adult but not saying or doing. When he does begin to answer her, he is likely first to imitate the motion. He may start with a tiny lift of his hand almost as though he doesn't even know he's doing it. Or maybe he'll flutter his fingers in his lap. He won't learn the word and the gesture at the same time. Some babies learn the word first and then raise their hand while others wave before they speak the word. He decides for himself, and it's some weeks before he does both together.

WHY GOAL: To provide a model for your child by waving and saying "hi" and "bye-bye."

USES: A child who receives a pleasant response to his actions will try to repeat those actions. Because the gestures are universal, they provide him with an opportunity to communicate with those not familiar with his own unique "family" language.

27. "Hi" and "Bye-bye"

HOW Treat your baby like any other friend. Say "hi" and wave when you come close to him. Wave bye-bye when you're leaving. Nothing will seem to happen for a long while. But, you'll feel almost as proud as he does when one day he smiles and waves back.

WHY To wave and say "hi" and "bye-bye" so your child will too

28. Providing Two Ways

HOW ADULT: A *box* that you can make with a small hole in the top and a larger hole in one side can provide many enjoyable problem-solving sessions for you and your baby. Using one *small object*, show the child that it can be dropped through the hole in the top. If he doesn't begin to look for the toy, ask, "Can you see it? Can you get it?" If he tries to get it through the small hole where his hand will not go, turn and tilt the box slightly to help him see the toy through the side. □ Naturally, you'll want to reduce your help as he begins to gain skill at the game. Using another small object take turns at the game pretending the object's disappeared and being surprised and delighted at finding it again. Your sharing the fun and repeating his actions can show the child that what he's doing is respected. When he learns the game, you may find it satisfying to step back and let him play it alone with several "drop" toys.

CHILD: The child may not want to drop the toy at first because he's not sure he'll get it back. He may try to look into and reach into the small hole where he last saw the toy. As he discovers the easier way, he will more frequently go directly to that. He may even begin to watch through the bigger hole for the toy to drop down into sight. In his effort to get the toy he may turn the box around or crawl around it to find the large hole. Some babies will play until the adults are exhausted! Perhaps that's because there's something very satisfying to the baby about having complete mastery and control over a process.

WHY GOAL: To help the child know that things are still there even when they drop out of sight. To provide experience in problem solving.

USES: Solving a problem usually involves choosing from several possible courses of action. Helping the infant to look for and discover alternative solutions in the problem of disappearing objects will provide him with models for action in solving more complex problems.

28. Providing Two Ways

HOW Give the child a box with a small hole in the top. He will enjoy dropping a toy into the hole. Ask him to find it again. Then help him discover the larger hole in the side that gives another way for him to get the toy. Use words such as, "It's not gone. You found it some other place. You got it out all by yourself."

WHY To provide experience in solving the problem of where things go

29. Puzzle Play

HOW ADULT: Any time you can find an object that will easily fit into a hole—you have something that might provide your baby with a start at puzzle play. If you have a sink with an old-fashioned rubber *stopper*, he might enjoy putting it in and out—as if the stopper were a puzzle piece. □ Look around the house for some things that will "just fit" into the cup depressions of a *muffin tin*. The fit needs to be fairly snug so it feels like a puzzle. (For example, ping-pong-sized *balls* will fit nicely into some of the smaller muffin tins.) When you're ready for a little learning fun together, sit down with your child and the "puzzle." Let him explore with the parts while you observe and make a few comments such as, "You put it in . . . you made it fit just right. Will another one fit in this hole?" If he gets interested in bouncing the balls or something besides the puzzle, follow his lead and make a learning game out of that. The puzzle can wait. Using a muffin tin is an easy first step because there's no right and wrong hole—they're all the same size. □ But later you can go a step further by tracing around two round *biscuit cutters* of different sizes on a shoe *box lid* and cutting out the shapes with scissors. When you sit down with this new puzzle (perhaps after the child is developmentally a year old), you will be able to say with pleasure, "Yes, you put the big one in the big hole. Where does the little one go?"

CHILD: The baby loves to poke his fingers into holes. He may explore a depression with his hands before thinking about fitting another object into it. He will enjoy holding onto the little handles of the cookie and biscuit cutters. Many babies will take the puzzle pieces apart immediately after putting them together. They're not interested in "finishing" it—but simply will it go together? Will it come apart?

WHY GOAL: To provide some things that will be enjoyable for the baby to fit together. To observe the child and increase the challenge of eye-hand coordination.

USES: In this game the child gains skill in judging sizes and shapes with his eyes and testing them with his hands. Puzzles come in such a wide range of difficulty that their enjoyment can stretch indefinitely into the child's future.

29. Puzzle Play

HOW You can invent a first puzzle for your baby. Find things that can "fit together," such as some balls and a small muffin pan. See if the baby will fit the balls into the holes. Or let him put one or two dull-edge biscuit cutters into holes cut in a shoe box lid. You can give him the enjoyment of many "puzzles" that are just right for each age.

WHY To add gradually to the challenge and enjoyment of an eye-hand game

30. Showing to Share

HOW ADULT: After your baby is four months old or so, he probably can focus on things across the room. Begin to let him know you're on the way by talking as you come into the room and showing him what you're bringing. After you've spoken, pause a second to give him a chance to locate you and turn his head toward you; then hold up his *bottle* and say, "Here's your bottle. Would you like me to feed you?" He can have time to anticipate and get ready for what is going to happen. ☐ When you're dressing him, take a second to show him his pretty *shirt* before you pull it on. Don't limit the experience to caretaking routines. Look for things that you enjoy and hold them in your hand for him to see. Showing is a simple experience that doesn't end when the child learns to talk but carries into adulthood as a universal way or sharing that requires no language. ☐ Until he is more mobile, bring bits of the world to show him. Show him the *vase* you're dusting, the pretty *peach* on his baby food jar, a *leaf* you've picked up. A mother might show him her sparkling *earrings* before putting them on. You're showing him not only an interesting sight but that you care enough about him to share the things that please you.

CHILD: The child will begin to understand what comes next when he sees a familiar object. But more than that, he will begin to sense the love that prompts the adult to share something with him. He may at first just look and maybe respond with a smile, but soon he'll develop his own unique ways of demonstrating he's interested. In time he may begin to hold up a toy he's playing with to share with the adult who comes near and look at her face to see what her reaction is.

WHY GOAL: To widen the child's visual experience. To interact socially with the child through the technique of showing.

USES: Showing (or sharing an object visually) is good preparation for the time in which objects are shared by actually relinquishing them for a time to the other person.

30. Showing to Share

HOW Call your baby from across the room. When he looks toward you, show him the bottle you're going to give him. He will have time to get ready for it. As you go about, share pretty things with him by holding them up for him to see. Show him the keys to the car before you go for a ride.

WHY To widen the child's experience by making sure he sees things you are sharing

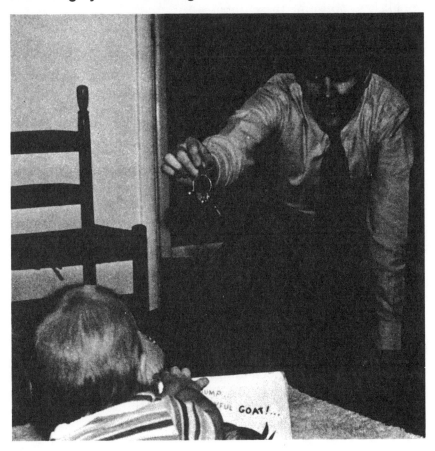

31. Things to Taste

HOW ADULT: Babies put everything in their mouths because tasting is one of the ways they find out about things. After they've tasted and handled, they decide whether they like it or not. (For this game the baby should have at least two upper and two lower teeth.) □ When she is comfortable, put some objects such as a *slice of banana*, a *spoon*, a *peeled apple slice* or pieces of *cracker* where she can reach them easily, perhaps on her feeding table. Let her choose what she wants and let her taste as long as she wants. (She's not likely to consume these things—just mouth them.) Approve of her choice by talking about it: "That's a juicy apple," "The spoon is smooth and cool." □ When she's older and you notice her peeping under things, put her at a table with a *cupcake pan* filled with several things of different textures and odors, such as a few drops of *honey*, a bit of *ice pop*, a slice of *orange* without seeds, or a spoonful of *pudding*. Lay a *plastic lid* over each cup. Encourage her to lift the lids and try the contents. Observe and respond with words such as "sweet," "cold," "wet," as she takes the lead, moving from one taste to the other and back again.

CHILD: The child will probably pop the first thing she touches into her mouth. She may drop it and try something else immediately or she may be interested in only that one thing for a while. She'll just pick randomly at the beginning but will become more selective as she is given repeated opportunities. She may need help in getting away from some of the stickier things. But that won't keep her from being just as curious about tastes as she is about most things that come her way.

WHY GOAL: To help the child learn differences using several senses together. To encourage curiosity by giving the child interesting choices.

USES: Besides providing encouragement to the child's curiosity by letting her choose from among several tastes, you're establishing positive attitudes toward new eating experiences and preparing her for self-feeding.

31. Things to Taste

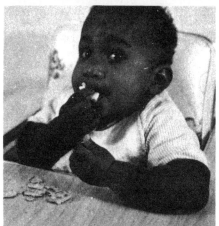

HOW Let your baby's love of tasting help her learn to make choices. Make her comfortable at her table and lay some things on it to taste. Let her taste whatever she picks up. Talk to her about the squashy banana or the smooth spoon as she sucks on them. Don't worry about the mess she makes. Keep it pleasant—you want her to feel it's good to try tasting new things. Later, put some things to taste in a cupcake pan covered with light plastic lids.

WHY To help the child learn differences using the senses of taste and touch together

> **Safety note:** Be sure to give only things you are confident your child will not choke on. If you're unsure, save this activity until your child is older.

32. Hiding a Picture

HOW ADULT: This memory game gives the child a chance to use his crawling skills. The child and adult sit together on the floor. The adult shows the child a *box* with a large *picture* attached, of a baby or some other familiar thing. She talks about the picture saying things like, "Look at the baby. The baby's smiling." She allows plenty of time for the child to get to know the picture and responds to his curiosity—"You're patting the baby." She then turns the box until the picture is just out of the child's sight and asks, "Where's the baby?" If he doesn't look for the baby, she turns it back and talks some more. □ The second time she turns it away, she keeps tapping on the picture and makes sure the child follows with his eyes. When he does look for it and finds it, she lets him know he's done a difficult thing. After playing every day for a week with one picture, the adult adds another picture to a second side of the box and asks the child to find first one and then the other in turn. This game can be made challenging enough to be stretched out over a full month by spending a week with two pictures, another week with three, and another with four pictures.

CHILD: The child may look at the picture, "talk" to it, and touch it. After it is turned, he may at first be puzzled. Encouraging words help him to understand it's somewhere. He may then reach toward the box and flip it around or crawl around the box to see. After two or more pictures have been added, he must make a choice. Now the words he's been hearing will be the clues that tell him which picture to choose.

WHY GOAL: To enable the crawling child to independently recover an interesting sight that has disappeared. To use language to help the child remember and choose.

USES: The child will begin to associate the words with the picture. At first he needs both picture and words, but later, hearing the words will bring to mind the picture if he has seen it a few seconds before. As his memory develops, more time can pass between his seeing and recalling. (Doesn't this seem a little like what you do when you flip through a magazine looking for an article you meant to go back and read?)

32. Hiding a Picture

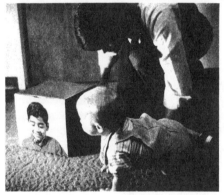

HOW Have some fun with your baby playing a "memory" game. Sit with him on the floor where he can crawl. Show him a box with a big picture of something he knows. Turn the picture away and ask him to find it again. When the picture is out of sight, remind him by using the name of the picture. Give him all the help he needs, but let the success be his.

WHY To use language to help the child remember what to search for

33. Letting Him Choose

HOW Adult: When the child knows what an object such as a *spoon* or a bar of *soap* or a *cup* is used for, the adult can encourage him to make some choices. When he is ready to drink, she shows him an empty cup and a full one; to eat, she shows him a spoon and a *popsicle stick* (or maybe even a *jar lid*); to wash, she shows him a *block* and a piece of soap; to take a walk, she shows him a *hat* and a *towel*. □ If he does not make the reasonable choice, she lets him try to drink from the empty cup; eat with the lid; rub his hands with the block; put the towel on his head. She laughs gently with him about the funny things that happen. □ Again, she shows him the two objects and encourages him to choose more appropriately. At another time she might just lay two things down and let him choose, being careful to praise him when he chooses reasonably. She is wise not to choose a second object that is so attractive he's interested only in playing with it.

Child: At first the child may choose the thing that is not useful. He may try to use it anyway and make a game of it for a while. When he finds the proper thing is more useful to him, he will probably begin to choose that one intentionally. □ Some babies seem already to have a sense of humor and they might enjoy the fun of being silly with the wrong thing more than getting on with the business of using the correct thing. The adult can relax and have fun with him and think about sensible choices another time.

WHY Goal: To help the child make choices. To provide the child with an opportunity for selecting the tool that is most useful for a particular task.

Uses: Choosing between two objects on the basis of their usefulness is an early step in the process of learning how to evaluate. Logical selection requires some knowledge on the part of the child as to what the objects can do and what his needs are in relation to the task at hand. Bringing the two ideas together is an important synthesis.

33. Letting Him Choose

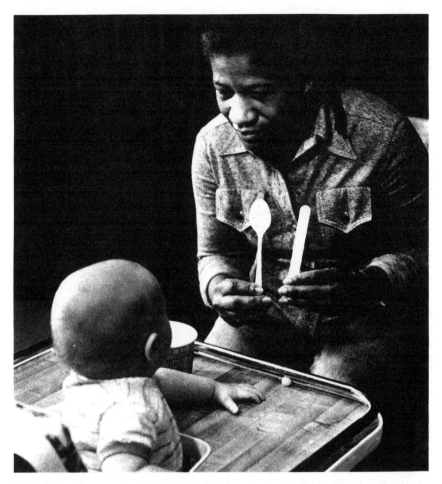

HOW Interesting things can happen when you give the baby a chance to make choices. Instead of just putting his spoon beside his cereal bowl, hold it up with another thing like a popsicle stick. Let him choose what he needs. Whichever he chooses, he gets to try to eat with it. Laugh with him about the silly things that happen when he chooses the stick. Encourage him to choose again. Give him other choices to make.

WHY To give the child a chance to select the tool that is most useful for the task

34. Introducing Crayons

HOW ADULT: The adult tapes a large piece of *paper* on the table at which the child is seated. She then offers a *crayon* that has had the covering removed and gives him some time to get to know what it is. He may taste it, feel it, or show it to the adult. She talks about "crayon," "smooth," "blue" and whatever will answer his curiosity about the crayon. □ In the handling he is likely to make a mark on the paper. If he doesn't, the adult can take another crayon and demonstrate what he might do. When he makes a mark, she says such things as, "Look at that," or "You put a mark on the paper!" She does not expect him to draw "things." □ At the beginning the child is given only one crayon. Later he is allowed to choose his own from several the adult holds. He should have used crayons many times before he is left with a large collection to choose from. Taping the paper to the table leaves him free to use the crayon in either hand. If he wants to draw on the furniture, she shows him that the crayon is for use only on the paper.

CHILD: The child will examine the crayon to see what can be done with it. He will probably put it in his mouth, but he'll be less interested in eating it after he finds more exciting ways to use it. □ His first marks will be more accidental than intentional. He may make long strokes or just jab at the paper. He's enjoying moving his arm and hand and he's seeing that something happens when he does. It will be some time before he sets out to make a particular line with the crayon.

WHY GOAL: To start the baby using crayons as a positive introduction to tools in general. To provide an opportunity for self-expression.

USES: Crayons and other markers provide a means for a great deal of independent exploration at the child's present age. As he grows older, like all people he will do some things with tools (like writing) that are not possible without tools.

34. Introducing Crayons

HOW Let your child make some marks in his world. Tape down a big piece of paper and give him a crayon. He may taste it and feel it before he marks with it. He won't draw things. He will just see what the crayon can do. Let him know how you feel, saying, "I'm glad you're using the crayon."

WHY To start the baby on the use of an important tool

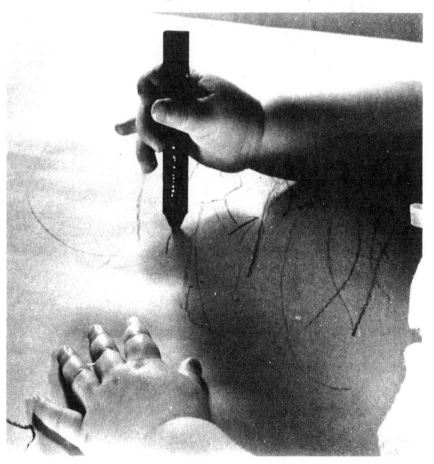

12-18 Months

Walking does more for the child than provide a new way to get from one place to another. Standing up and moving about seem to make the child more aware of himself as a unique and separate individual. He begins to take an interest in his own needs: helping with dressing and undressing, holding his own cup, and trying to use a spoon.

Now that he's discovered walking, the infant looks for other new ways to move. Most toddlers happily find that they can climb steps, stoop and get up, kneel, and walk backward. This constant locomotion can be wearing for the adult, but delight and pride help keep life on an even keel.

At this stage it sometimes seems that language does not develop at its earlier promised rate. Perhaps language is temporarily given a back seat for some infants because so much energy and attention are being given to physical movement.

If decisions about limits for the child's exploration have not been made by this stage, it is a good time for the adults to think about their own needs in relation to the child's and to make some rules for him and some adjustments in their own daily pattern of living. Reasonable and understandable rules help add smoothness to family life and will not get in the way of playfulness and affection.

TABLE OF CONTENTS

THEMES

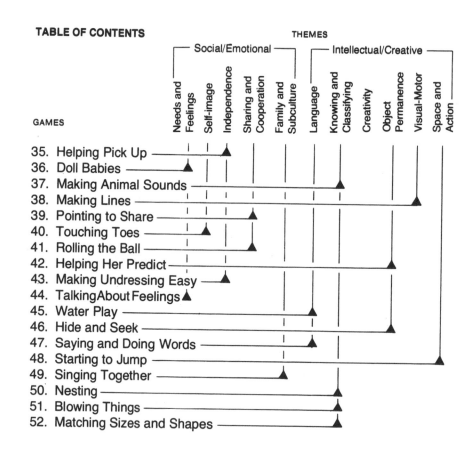

GAMES	Social/Emotional					Intellectual/Creative					
	Needs and Feelings	Self-image	Independence	Sharing and Cooperation	Family and Subculture	Language	Knowing and Classifying	Creativity	Object Permanence	Visual-Motor	Space and Action
35. Helping Pick Up			▲								
36. Doll Babies	▲										
37. Making Animal Sounds							▲				
38. Making Lines										▲	
39. Pointing to Share				▲							
40. Touching Toes		▲									
41. Rolling the Ball				▲							
42. Helping Her Predict									▲		
43. Making Undressing Easy			▲								
44. Talking About Feelings	▲										
45. Water Play						▲					
46. Hide and Seek									▲		
47. Saying and Doing Words							▲				
48. Starting to Jump											▲
49. Singing Together						▲					
50. Nesting							▲				
51. Blowing Things							▲				
52. Matching Sizes and Shapes							▲				

78

Checklist: 12-18 Months
(Developmental Age)

NEW BEHAVIORS	SUGGESTED GAMES	NEW BEHAVIORS	SUGGESTED GAMES
☐ Cooperates in games involving imitation	35	☐ Shows interest in things or games other children like	46
☐ Holds, hugs, and spanks dolls	36	☐ Points to at least one body part when asked (on self or doll)	47
☐ Imitates and echoes words and sounds	37		
☐ Scribbles spontaneously	38	☐ Imitates adult's crayon strokes (a fast, more or less straight mark across page)	
☐ Points to show desires and call attention to events	39		
☐ Shows where his toes, eyes, and nose are	40	☐ Tries to stand on a flat board	48
☐ Throws ball intentionally	41	☐ Brings something from or takes something to another place	
☐ Walks up stairs with help			
☐ Pitches or brings objects in direction he wants	42	☐ Begins to hum and sing	49
☐ Takes off socks or shoes (if unfastened)	43	☐ Keeps himself busy and happy for at least fifteen minutes with building, looking at pictures, or other similar activity	50
☐ Uses a spoon without help and with very little spilling			
☐ Uses some sounds (words and wordlike sounds) to tell feelings	44		
☐ Knows and says the names of at least five things	45	☐ Puffs air (enough to blow out candle)	51
		☐ Puts round block in round hole	52

35. Helping Pick Up

HOW ADULT: When the child has been playing with the *toys* from his box and he is beginning to tire of them, invite him to help you pick them up. Sit beside him, show him a *pickup container* (such as a *plastic dishpan*), and drop one of the toys in, talking pleasantly about what you're doing. Hand him a toy and ask him to put it in. If he doesn't, take it gently from him and drop it in the container to show him what you mean. Then take it out, hand it to him again, and again ask him to drop it in the pan. When he does, tell him what a good thing he did—to drop it in. □ Let him find another toy to "drop in." Naturally, you won't expect him to pick up the toys alone. At first he may pick up only one or two, which he will want to choose himself. If he wants to put something unreasonable in the container, give him an alternative place for it. Let him have additional opportunities for choosing by showing you which toy he wants you to put in next. You can make this a special time of sharing together and he'll learn that taking care of his own things is a pleasant thing to do—not an unhappy chore. Let him be a part of a game, not the only one playing it.

CHILD: The child will learn quickly to follow the adult's lead in dropping the toys in the pan, though before he understands he may want to take them out almost as fast as he puts them in. He may want to put just one toy in and out, but he'll begin to understand as he's guided by the adult's words and actions. When he's allowed some choice and his choice is approved, he may be a very willing partner.

WHY GOAL: To give him a chance to make choices in a routine care situation. To help the child feel good about himself by caring for some of his own needs.

USES: Helping with self-care tasks leads to independent behavior. When the choices he makes at simple tasks are approved, he gains trust in his own ability to make decisions—an important aspect of independence.

35. Helping Pick Up

HOW Make toy pickup time a game the two of you play together. Let him choose which toys he puts in the container. At first he will pick up only a couple. Let it be a pleasant sharing time so he can learn to feel good taking care of his own things.

WHY To give him a chance to make choices in a routine care situation

36. Doll Babies

HOW ADULT: The adult gives the child a *blanket* and *bottle* to use with her *baby doll*. After she's played a while, he might ask, "What does your baby need? Is baby hungry?" He talks about the bottle if she doesn't use it and shows her how if she needs help. He doesn't fuss about doing things a certain way. □ As she plays, he helps her to think about the doll's needs by relating them to her own experiences. "The baby's cold. What will make you and him warm?" "It makes you happy to rock your baby, doesn't it?" It's even more meaningful if the child plays with the doll while the adult is caring for a real baby. He talks about how he's caring, saying, "My baby needs some milk. I'm going to give her a bottle. What does your baby need?" □ Letting a boy play with a doll is not making a girl of him. In playing with dolls, he is learning how to care for other people. All of us need to know this.

CHILD: The child enjoys handling and loving the baby. She's not very skilled, so her handling may be a little awkward, but she will probably use the clothes and bottle in appropriate ways. She'll treat it at times like a person and at other times like a toy, carrying it around by its arm or foot. She'll like having it where she can play with it when she likes.

WHY GOAL: To provide a way for the child to come to a clearer understanding of her own feelings and needs. To help the child begin to think about the needs of others.

USES: Understanding your own feeling is a lifelong process. Babies act out all their feelings because they have few other ways of expressing them. Providing for the needs of others helps them in defining their own emotional needs and prepares them for later expressing those needs through both language and actions.

36. Doll Babies

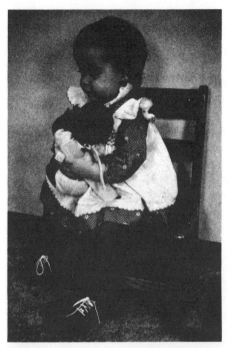

HOW Help your child think about her doll's needs—"Is your baby hungry? Does your baby need a blanket?" As you thoughtfully care for your child, she'll gain understanding of how to care for her "baby."

WHY To help the child begin thinking about the needs of others

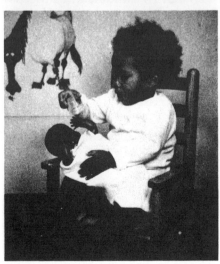

37. Making Animal Sounds

HOW ADULT: The adult names one of the child's *animal toys* and makes the sound the animal makes. "This is a dog. The dog says 'wuf.'" He repeats this as the child plays, encouraging her to make dog sounds. He asks, "What does the dog say?" The adult hams it up a bit, sounding ferocious and gentle at various times as he wufs or growls, keeping in mind the important thing: having the child imitate sounds (and words if she's ready). Another time, they play the game with a new animal and sound. ☐ When the child has learned several animals and their sounds, the adult shows her a *picture* of one she knows. At the same time he shows her the toy animal, pointing to the picture and then touching the toy. Then the adult removes the toy and shows her the picture only, asking what sound it makes. If she needs help, he says, "This is the cat. Can you remember what the cat says?" They continue to have fun with the game, using other pictures.

CHILD: The child may think the noises very funny and laugh at the adult. Soon she'll try. She may sound a little odd at first but it's fun, so she's eager to keep trying. (At this stage a few children will be ready to name the toy as well as imitate it.) ☐ When she first sees the pictures, the child may touch parts of the picture, then touch the same parts on the toy. When she understands the picture is the animal, she'll be quick to play the sound game with the picture.

WHY GOAL: To help the child recognize familiar animals and imitate their sounds. To help her understand that pictures stand for things.

USES: Playing the same imitation game of sound and sight with an object and its picture leads to a richer understanding of the picture as a representation of the object.

37. Making Animal Sounds

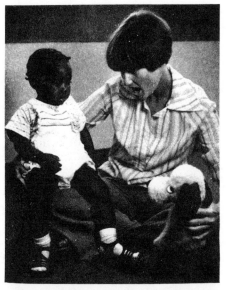

HOW Use the baby's love for animal toys to help her learn new sounds. Show her an animal toy. Name it and make a noise like it makes. Get her to try. When she can make the sound, show her a picture of the animal. Ask what the animal in the picture says. You'll enjoy each other's funny noises and the fun of talking together.

WHY To help the child "put together" familiar animals, their sounds, and their pictures

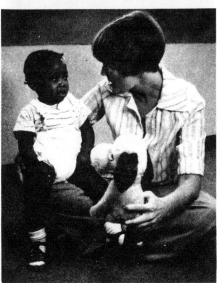

38. Making Lines

HOW ADULT: When you notice the baby tracing her finger over a flat surface, respond by telling her what she is doing. "You're making a wiggly line." Trace your finger beside her line and tell her you're making a wiggly line like hers. When the two of you are by a *steamy window* or *dusty table*, trace lines there. Talk about the lines with words that tell what they are: "That's a straight line," or "That one's curved." □ Show her how to spread her fingers apart and make a series of lines or to ball her fingers into a fist and make a wide stroke. Outside she can use a *stick* to trace in the *sand* or in the *mud*. Encourage her to use her fingers in many ways. □ In bringing her attention to the shapes of the lines, you are helping her to see the differences she has accidentally made happen. She will be ready to make these same differences happen purposefully when she gains more hand control.

CHILD: Children enjoy making marks. Perhaps it's because they see immediately that they can make things happen. When she's marking with you, the child knows it's an all-right thing and she's freer to try new ways. As you talk about the lines and as she feels her arm making the lines, she's becoming aware of details. But all that's unimportant to her right now. As far as she's concerned, she's just having fun. That's a good attitude for both of you.

WHY GOAL: To give the child varied experiences in making and noticing lines. To point out differences to her. .

USES: Noticing differences in lines is a basic form of visual discrimination. Practice in making lines helps her to feel differences as well as see them. The awareness she's gaining will be needed when she begins to use her hands for more complex tasks such as controlled scribbling, drawing or writing.

38. Making Lines

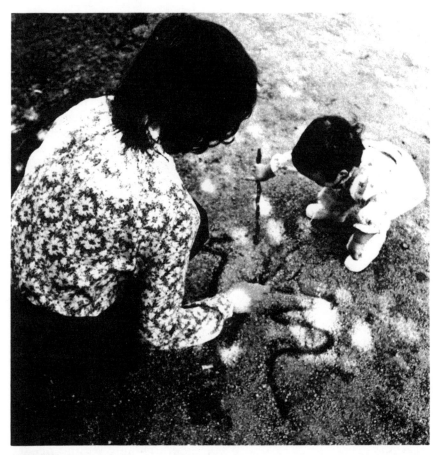

HOW Find places for you and your child to make some lines with your fingers or with a stick. Talk about the lines. "You made a wiggly line in the mud." She will begin to notice differences, too. You'll enjoy seeing how many things she can make.

WHY To help the child become more aware of the many kinds of marks she can make with her hands

39. Pointing to Share

HOW ADULT: When the child becomes mobile and is able to approach more things on her own, share some of the new things in her world by pointing to them. When she's looking for her ball, point . . . "There's your ball," . . . and let her see it for herself. □ At the beginning you might walk over and touch the ball to help her understand because when you begin to point, the baby will most likely look at the end of your finger rather than the place you're pointing to. Give her a visual path to follow by using your whole arm in a broad gesture (as if you were throwing or bowling) and ending by unfolding your finger to point. Her eyes will follow the movement of your arm and on past your finger to the spot you want her to see. □ When she has learned to read your gesture, share with her things she might not see on her own. Point high to clouds or airplanes or leaves blowing; far to lights or signs or people walking. Help her see the things you enjoy, the birds at the feeder or a simple flower. When she needs things, share your knowledge of where they are by pointing them out to her.

CHILD: At first the child looks at the adult's hand, maybe because that's where things have often been before. After the adult walks over and touches the objects a few times or uses broad gestures for her to follow, she begins to understand that pointing is giving her the direction. Very quickly she seems to know she can share her own discoveries by pointing, and some babies say their first simple sentence as an accompaniment to pointing at some particularly exciting thing they want everyone to share. "See pretty lights!" or "Look, Daddy."

WHY GOAL: To share with your baby things that neither of you is holding. To enjoy a social interaction.

USES: Understanding that pointing indicates a direction provides the child with a means of communicating about things that are not close enough to touch.

39. Pointing to Share

HOW Show your baby things by pointing to them. Move your whole arm as you point in the direction you want her to look. She'll follow the motion of your arm instead of just looking at the end of your finger. You can share the sight of distant things or big things like trees and airplanes that you cannot hold for her to see.

WHY To enjoy helping the child learn about things that are "out of hand"

40. Touching Toes

HOW ADULT: When the child is beginning to name things, play this game with her to help her know words about herself. Touch your own ears, saying to the child, "I'm touching my ears, can you touch your ears?" Give the child time and repeat if she needs it. □ When things are going well, use words that the child usually doesn't hear—elbows, shin, ankles, back, etc.—and encourage her to say them in the game. If the child touches a new part of her body, name that part as you imitate her actions. □ Singing a song with the game makes it even more exciting for her. Use song games you've learned as a child that involve doing things with various parts of the body, perhaps, a simple version of "Looby-Loo" or the "Hokey-Pokey." You can make up appropriate new verses as you go along. The two of you can make up new songs together.

CHILD: The child follows the lead of the adult though she may be slower in touching the right spot because she has to see where it is first. She'll understand the words long before she learns to say them and will be happy if the adult follows her lead sometimes. This gives her a chance to find the words for some parts of herself she's discovered. She'll learn to say the words faster if only a few parts are used each game time. Otherwise she'll be overwhelmed with too many new ideas and may give up.

WHY GOAL: To help the child learn words for the parts of her body as a way of knowing herself better.

USES: Labeling is an early stage in defining things. In labeling and defining the various parts of the body, the child is made more aware of herself as an individual.

40. Touching Toes

HOW Words can help your child know more about who she is. Play a touch-and-name game, saying, "Hands on your knees," "Touch your toes," "Put your fingers on your ears." She'll want to be the leader sometimes. You'll enjoy following her lead.

WHY To give the child words that help her know herself better

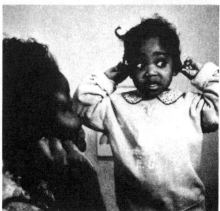

41. Rolling the Ball

HOW ADULT: The adult and child sit on the floor facing each other with their legs spread and feet touching to keep the ball from rolling away. The adult then rolls the *ball* in such a way that the child is sure to catch it. The child may be reluctant to give it up. The adult talks to her about rolling it back "so I can roll it to you again." If she still refuses, the adult can take it gently from her and then roll it quickly back. □ When the adult has repeated this several times, the child can see that she is not losing the ball when she rolls it away. The short distance between them and the way they are sitting makes catching easy. The adult makes sure by the way she plays that the child is successful because she knows it's important for the child to feel good about playing with another person. □ The adult is helping the child to understand that some things work better with a partner and that in a partnership you must give sometimes (throw) in order to get back (catch).

CHILD: The child may at first want to throw the ball, but she's more likely to want to keep it. Holding the ball all by yourself isn't much fun, so when she learns she'll get it back, she enters into the game. Her catching skills may at first just be picking up the ball after it stops rolling. The fun is in having a pleasant time with someone she likes. As her skill increases, the distance can be made greater. This is a game she'll enjoy playing with a friend or a big brother after they have both learned the give-and-take that's necessary to keep the game fun.

WHY GOAL: To teach a very easy form of "cooperation" in an enjoyable game.

USES: Knowing how to do things cooperatively will prepare the way for the child to enter into more complex kinds of play.

41. Rolling the Ball

HOW Be a partner to your child in a ball game. Roll a soft ball back and forth to each other. She'll learn the give-and-take that goes with being partners. You'll have fun seeing her learn yet another new thing.

WHY To play a game with simple rules that will introduce her to cooperation

42. Helping Her Predict

HOW ADULT: Adults can play a game that helps the child guess where an object might be after it's disappeared. The adult finds a *soft ball* and a *big box*. He stands with the child several feet from the box and throws the ball into it. He asks the child, "Where did it go. Do you see it?" If the child doesn't understand, he encourages her to look in the box. He lets the child be the one to "find" it and is very pleased and happy when she does. They again step away from the box and the child is invited to throw the ball. Each time the adult acts surprised and pleased when the ball's found. □ The game can be played another way with a ball and *tube*. The adult sits at one end and rolls the ball through the tube to the child and encourages the child to roll it back. She uses words such as "There it goes," "Here it comes," and "Through the tube." They find various ways to hold the tube that make the ball go slow or fast and give the game more excitement.

CHILD: To throw, the child must stand close enough to the box to get the ball into it but not close enough to see in. She can play alone after she has learned where to look for the ball, but she'll usually want to share the fun with the adult. □ When they play with the tube, the child may not at first expect the ball to come through. She'll try to look into the tube for it or pick up the tube to dump it out. After a few sessions she will start to expect it to come out the other end. She is now anticipating what will happen because it's happened before.

WHY GOAL: To give the child experience in predicting where an object will be that has gone out of sight. To help the child to expect things to happen.

USES: The understanding of object permanence enables the child to make rudimentary predictions. Knowing she can make certain things happen and can predict the results builds the child's self-trust.

42. Helping Her Predict

HOW Throw a ball into a big box. Invite the child to look for it. When she finds it, show you're as pleased as she is that it isn't gone forever. Roll a ball through a tube. Soon she'll look for it to come out the other end. You're helping her to feel secure by knowing what is going to happen.

WHY To give the child experience in predicting where an object will be

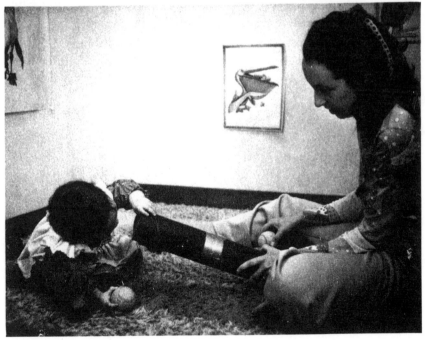

43. Making Undressing Easy

HOW ADULT: The adult helps with undressing by planning plenty of time and by making it easy. The child usually shows interest in his shoes first. Untie the child's shoes, loosen the lacing, and pull the shoe over the heel so the child has only to pull it off the toe. □ Socks are taken off the same way. Of course it's easier for adults to go ahead and take off the shoes and socks, but it is important that the child learn to do it for himself. When the child does pull his shoe off, praise him even though he only lifts it off his toes. □ When he's ready to try more difficult pieces of clothing, unfasten the coat or shirt and help by pulling one sleeve off. Show the child how to hold the other sleeve at the cuff and pull it off. Help with pants by having the child stand until the pants are pushed to his knees, then sit to pull them over his feet by himself. □ Encourage the child to do as much for himself as he can. As the child is learning to take off his shoes and shirt, help him use the words . . . "shirt, shoes" . . . and include them in your praise of what he did. Adults must be prepared to do a lot of waiting while the child tries for himself.

CHILD: The child may want to help undress himself before he can really do much. He may get upset when he can't take something off but still not want anybody else to do it. He will usually be willing to try a new way if it makes him feel he did it himself. As he learns that he can do some by himself, he will be more willing to accept help with the rest.

WHY GOAL: To loosen the child's clothes and arrange them so he can start being partly independent now.

USES: Undressing is a basic part of caring for one's own needs and is a step toward independence. Ability to undress is usually acquired before the ability to dress.

43. Making Undressing Easy

HOW Help your baby to undress himself. Get his clothes ready so he can do the easy part. Untie his shoes and loosen the heels. Help him with the sleeves so he can pull the shirt over his head. Lots and lots of patience will enable you both to enjoy his learning.

WHY To loosen clothes so the child can finish "by himself"

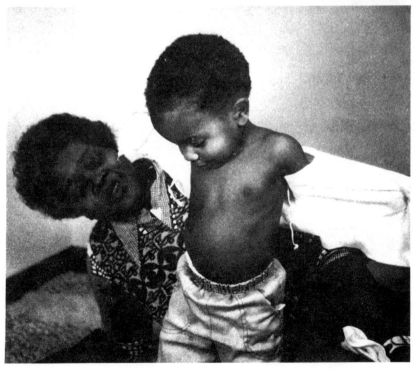

44. Talking About Feelings

HOW ADULT: When your baby was quite young you made a point of letting her see feelings expressed on your face. Now you can help her by giving her words as well as facial expressions. Watch for those occasions that are special and her feelings very strong, then give her a word to express it. When she's first walked across the room: "Walking makes you very proud doesn't it?" When she makes one of her first crayon marks: "You're excited to see what you and the crayon can do." When she 'finds' in hide and seek: "Wow, you were really surprised when you found me." □ Help her with words at other times too. When she's annoyed because the shoe won't come off, help her to say so. You need to help her to remember that she can use words instead of actions sometimes: "Be calm, use your voice to tell me." And give her some words for the calm times too, "happy" when she's rocking, "pleased" when she's finished her task, and "big" when she's done it herself.

CHILD: The child is doing many new things now and she needs lots of help to understand the feelings that go with all these new activities. It will be a long time before she knows clearly what the feelings are and a long time before she knows all the right words. But she is learning that words can be used. She might learn one and use it for all her feelings for a while. She may say she's angry when she's frightened or annoyed or just feeling bad, but she's using language to express and trusting you to interpret and have patience until she gets things straight.

WHY GOAL: To show the child that words can help to tell what she's feeling.

USES: The child, who must live with other people as well as herself, needs to discover socially accepted ways of expressing those feelings she has in common with the rest of humanity. Hearing and recognizing her feelings expressed in a trusted adult's language precedes the expression of those feelings in the child's language. When she has words for her feelings, the child will have a choice between words and actions for expression. Both are good.

44. Talking About Feelings

HOW Try to understand how your baby is feeling and give her some words to express it: "You feel very big when you're walking," or "It's exciting to see the bubbles flying." She may give you a big smile to show how happy she is that you can share her feelings.

WHY To show the child that words as well as actions can help to tell what she is feeling

45. Water Play

**Here are some ideas
for your language about
water play.**

"tickly"
"squirting"
"taste"
"pool"
"shovel"
"splashes"

"cold tap"
"dripping"
"in the cup"
"warm water"
"wet cloth"
"soft towel"

45. Water Play

HOW Let bath time be relaxed for you and the child. Talk a lot about the soap and cloth and toys—how they feel in the water and what they do. Follow the child's lead and give him the words as he needs them. Also play outdoors with the child and his friends.

WHY To let the child hear words for what he does and what he is touching

"holding the hose"
"in a stream"
"slippery hose"
"warm skin"
"helping"
"slippery walk"
"splashes"
"bubbles"
"in the water"

46. Hide and Seek

HOW ADULT: Tell the child you are going to hide, then duck down behind a chair or move around a doorway into another room, letting her see you go, and hiding so she can see part of you. Call, "Can you find me?," "Where am I?" When she does find you, be very excited and pleased she did. Say "boo" and grab her up for a big hug. □ Play again, hiding in new places as long as you're both having fun. Invite her to hide, asking "Where is Carla?" When you find her, be very surprised and hug her close as you tell her you're glad you "found her again." □ When the child is a little older, hide a toy in another room. Show the child a big teddy bear or doll and tell her you're going to hide it. Then go out of the room or out of sight behind a wall and put the teddy bear down where the child will be able to see it easily. Don't let her see you hide it. Go back to where she is and ask, "Where is teddy? Can you help me find him?" If the child doesn't understand, give her hints, "Is it in there in the kitchen?" Point or give any help the child needs, even walking with her into the room if necessary. Of course, you're very surprised when you find it. Look for ways to play as you care for her. Say things like, "Where are your milk and cookies? Can you find where I put them for you?"

CHILD: When she begins to hide, she will probably use the same place the adult has just hidden. She'll laugh, stamp her feet and clap when the hider jumps out, or when she's found. She may come popping out from all kinds of unexpected places. Then finding something she didn't see hidden will be a new step. □ Children of all ages all over the world play this game, which is a good indication of how much your child will enjoy it. (If your family has a different version, she'll enjoy playing it the way your parents showed you.)

WHY GOAL: To help the child independently find something that is out of sight. To introduce your child to the pleasure of Hide and Seek.

USES: Learning to look for things she can't see gives the child a new tool for problem solving. Discovering through the universal game of Hide and Seek makes her akin to children in all cultures.

46. Hide and Seek

HOW Hide something new for your baby to find—yourself, for example. Stoop behind a chair where she can still see part of you. Call, "Can you find me?" Have a cuddle with her when she does. After a while, she may want to hide. Be really glad to see her again when you "find" her. Later help Mr. Bear hide.

WHY To encourage the child to rely on her own ability to find something hidden

47. Saying and Doing Words

HOW ADULT: When the child is tumbling or rolling around the floor, the adult can imitate the movements and say what is happening: "We're rolling over," "You're standing on your head." He can suggest some new things and do them with the child, always giving the child words for what they're doing. "Make your hands go up and down. Bend over. Spread your arms wide." □ New movements that need a little more skill can be used as the child gets older and has more control of his body. Several children can play together with the adult. He asks the children to do and say what he does. Part of the game now is to say what you're going to do before you do it. □ Some possible movements are:

DO
1. stand on toes with arms high
2. squat, tuck in head, hold knees
3. play on ladder or hill
4. roll on carpet or grass

SAY
"stand tall"
"make a ball"

"climb up"
"roll over and over"

As a child learns more language, he can be the leader and say what to do.

CHILD: The child will be especially pleased when the adult follows his lead. The more active the game, the more the child will enjoy it. Learning the words comes more slowly than doing the motions, and the motions will be less than perfect. He may get very silly and tumble and roll around, but he will have great fun while learning.

WHY GOAL: To help attach labels to the child's actions so he will begin to learn the words for what he is doing.

USES: In the early stages of using words children sometimes have difficulty sorting out an action word from the object that performs the action. Acting out helps meaning become clearer.

47. Saying and Doing Words

HOW Join your child when he's rolling and tumbling. Give him some words for his actions. Help him do some new things by showing him and telling him. "Spread your arms wide" or "Stand on your head." Hug him and give him a big smile when he does what the words tell him.

WHY To help the child learn the words for what he is doing

48. Starting to Jump

HOW ADULT: Now that the child's walking well, adults can have some rollicking times showing him new ways he can move in space. The adult helps the child to stand balanced on a *low stool* or a *step*. Holding the child under the arms, the adult jumps him to the floor saying, "Jump." She lifts the child a little higher than necessary to help him feel the movement. □ After some practice the adult holds out her hands to the child and encourages him to jump. She lets the child maintain his own balance, but gives the child her hands for support. □ Another day the adult props one end of a *board* up several inches off the floor. She starts the child at the lower end of the board and encourages him to walk up it and step off the end. She uses the words "up" and "down" as the child walks, jumping him down at the end until he feels comfortable with this new game. □ Together they can think of other ways to play on the board. A game jumping "over" instead of "off" offers another challenge. The adult ties a *rope* between two chairs so that it is about an inch off the floor. She steps over it with a jumping motion, letting the child see her and saying the word "jump" as she goes. Then she takes the child's hand and asks him to jump with her. She lets the child try for himself when he's ready. □ Almost every family invents some special jumping games of its own. What are yours?

CHILD: At first, jumping is just stepping off, or over, for the child. Having a good romp with the adult is just as important as the jumping, and the child will be much more willing to try if it's all in a game. If he's not forced and is allowed to go when he's ready, he's likely to try most anything. (Some children need a little more time to get used to the idea, but if the stool and board or rope are left out for play, they'll try it sometimes by themselves.) Left to work at this movement by himself, he'll come to no harm. And if the adult is watching to reassure him after his little tumbles, he'll usually come up smiling.

WHY GOAL: To give the child a chance to jump and feel good about it. To help the child adjust to changes.

USES: In an environment planned for his safety and success, the child gains confidence for bigger tasks.

48. Starting to Jump

HOW Jumping is a new way for your child to move about. He will have great fun learning because you're playing with him. For some time he will just step off the stool or over the rope. He'll like trying for himself when you leave the stool or board out for him and watch from a distance.

WHY To give the child chances to jump and feel good about larger motions

49. Singing Together

HOW ADULT: When feeding, dressing, walking or riding, sing with your child. Make up your own or use traditional songs. You don't need to be a good singer as long as you enjoy it. If you want the child to sing along, choose a short simple tune or one in which you repeat certain words. The words don't have to make any particular sense, in fact nonsense songs are often favorites. □ Try to remember some that your father or mother sang to you. If you have a bilingual family, this is a great way to pass on some of the family's traditional language. Include the child's name in the song or sing about something that's happened to him or something he's doing. Try some with motions. □ Below are just a few samples of traditional songs:

EUROPEAN TRADITION
Go round and round the village,
Go round and round the village,
Go round and round the village,
As we have done before.

BLACK TRADITION
If anybody asks you who I am,
Who I am, Who I am,
If anybody asks you who I am,
Tell him I'm a child of God.

SPANISH TRADITION
Una boquita para comer,
Una naricita para oler,
Dos oidos para oir,
Y la cabecita para dormir.

CHILD: The child will at first listen then begin to make sounds with the adult. Soon he will be saying one or two words of the song at the appropriate time. It will be some time before he can start at the beginning and sing straight through, but that's okay because its just for fun. Even before he tries the words, he'll be clapping and moving to the tune and know the special feeling people share when they're having fun together.

WHY GOAL: To have fun with another person, your child. To help him learn words through the rhythm and repetition of singing them.

USES: Singing is a universal communication crossing all other language barriers. It provides the child with social and verbal experiences.

49. Singing Together

HOW Sing a lot with your baby. It will give your feelings a lift. Your baby will enjoy it and learn to sing with you. Make up some songs about what your baby's doing. Sing some songs your parents taught you.

WHY To have fun with another person and to teach words by singing them

50. Nesting

HOW ADULT: Household containers that come in graduated sizes (*juice cans, measuring cups,* or *plastic storage dishes*) have a built-in lesson to teach. You may try to stay in the background and see if a set of nonbreakable measuring cups will "suggest" anything to your toddler. □ When you're busy in the kitchen but she needs something to do, put the set of cups on the floor for her. Go on about your work but watch out of the corner of your eye what she's doing. Save your attention and comments for the times she nests two or more of the cups, "Look! You've got one inside the other." □ On another occasion you may want to structure the game a little more. Sit on the floor with the cups between the two of you. Place the largest cup upright and hold up two others. Ask, "Which one goes in next?" As she chooses one, tell what's happening: "Yes, that one went in. Now is there room for this other one?" It's perfectly reasonable to make mistakes, to take one out and try another, until they're arranged to the child's satisfaction. □ If she's not having much success, you might want to finish up the play session with a simpler version. Take away all the cups but three (the largest, middle-sized, and smallest) and invite her to nest these. It's always nice to end a Learningame with a loving hug and a sincere, "I like playing with you!"

CHILD: The toddler may find many things other than nesting to do with the measuring cups, juice cans, etc. She may first roll them, bang on them, hide things under them—who knows? In all of this she's still learning various kinds of things. But if the items fit together in an attractive and easy way, she is likely eventually to nest them.

WHY GOAL: To select and provide play materials that will draw the child's attention to graduated differences in size.

USES: A manipulative awareness of graded increases in size provides a small bit of progress toward the mathematical concept called seriation. This concept eventually enables us to understand ideas such as first, second, third, and so on.

50. Nesting

HOW Let the child put one thing inside another. She will begin to learn which is larger and which is smaller. Put some plastic measuring cups on the floor by her and enjoy seeing what she learns. If she doesn't fit one inside the other after a while, you might want to show her—but there's no hurry. Let your words tell what's happening. "You put the little one in . . . that's nice."

WHY To make it likely that the child will notice graduated differences in size

Easier

Harder

51. Blowing Things

HOW ADULT: Air can do fascinating things to other objects depending on their weight, size, and shape. Let the child try blowing to see what happens to lots of different things. □ Say, "Blow," and blow gently against the child's cheek or hair. Pucker your mouth and blow against a *tissue* so he can see you blow. Let him try. Help him: blow against a *feather*, blow ripples in *water*, blow a *plastic ball*, blow bits of *paper* away. □ Give him: a *straw*; a *whistle*; a *toy horn*; a *party blower*. Put several blowing toys in a box for the child to play with. Talk about blowing and blow through a horn, puffing out your cheeks so the child can see the sound being made. Be sure to have another interesting, quiet toy ready so when you've had enough of this "music," you can offer it to the child and put the box of whistles away until another time.

CHILD: The beginning blower is often a very sloppy blower! He may also suck in instead of blowing out. It's not as easy as it looks, and it may take some time before he can control whether he's blowing out or sucking in. □ When he's mastered the straw, he'll blow against everything within reach and be delighted to see bubbles forming or paper flying. The child loves blowing and he loves making noise, so he has double enjoyment with whistles and horns. Besides he's in control, and that's even more fun. He may find one whistle that sounds good to him (once he can make it work) and blow it for a long time, probably not tiring of it as soon as the adult does. He may even learn to blow with a rhythm if a radio or record player is turned on for him to "blow along" with.

WHY GOAL: To show the child how he can blow and make things happen. To help him see that different things react in different ways to the same stimulus.

USES: Repeating an event is an aspect of purposeful behavior. The child is encouraged to repeat an action if he discovers that the action can produce changes that are exciting. The child will need to continue confidently to explore what makes things happen in order to learn about his world.

51. Blowing Things

HOW All kinds of things happen when your child learns to blow. Blow gently on his cheek to help him feel the word "blow." Show him what to blow with: his mouth, a straw, a horn. Give him something to blow: bits of paper, water (with a little soap for bubbles), a cake with candles. It's so much fun you'll be joining him a lot of the time.

WHY To show the child another way he can make things happen

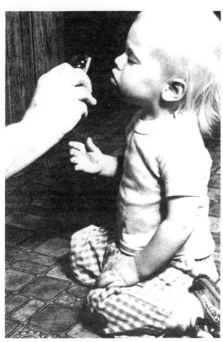

52. Matching Sizes and Shapes

HOW ADULT: This game will bring to the child's attention the sameness and differences in objects. *Three objects, two the same and one different* (like two spoons and a fork or two balls and a block) are given to the child to handle. When you observe the child feeling the objects and noticing their shapes, pick one up and talk about its identifying features. Show the child that two are the "same." Then pick up one of the two that are alike and hold it for him to see, in your hand. Say, "Get the one that's the same as this one." When he picks it up, put your hand beside his and touch the two objects. If he chooses the unlike one, name it, put it back, saying, "This other one is the same; see, it is rounded," "You found the one that is different." Clap your hands and show you're really pleased with him when he gets the right one. □ After matching shapes for a few days, you can change to matching sizes. Be sure to keep size and color constant when matching shapes and keep color and shape constant when matching sizes. □ Here are some ideas:

FOR MATCHING SHAPES: (color and size constant)
1. spoons and forks
2. elbow and shell macaroni
3. round and square plastic lids

FOR MATCHING SIZES: (color and shape constant)
1. big and little buttons
2. big socks little socks
3. big cans little cans

CHILD: The child will choose more purposefully when he begins to pay attention to the special features of the objects. When he begins the game, he may not understand what is expected of him and he may choose randomly. But he likes having the adult play with him, and it makes him feel good when she praises him and claps her hands when he chooses appropriately. So he begins to choose more deliberately, sometimes picking up the unlike one and putting it back as he sees it is different.

WHY GOAL: To help the child notice the size and shape features of an object that help identify it. To use the word "same."

USES: Noticing identifying features helps the child to use a new thing effectively because he will begin to know if it is like anything he has seen before.

52. Matching Sizes and Shapes

HOW Give the baby three objects of the same size and color. Two of them should be of the same shape (perhaps two spoons and a fork). Show him the spoons are the same— smooth, round. Show him how the fork is different—sharp, flat. Hold up one of the spoons and ask him to get the thing that's the same. Be really excited and pleased when he picks up the other spoon. At a later time play with new objects that are of different sizes but of the same shape and color. (Perhaps two little spoons and one big spoon).

WHY To help the child notice the parts of an object that help to identify it

Safety note: The adult must supervise closely when the child uses anything sharp, or small enough to go into an ear or nose or mouth.

18-24 Months

Serious investigation of everything is the full-time occupation of the year-and-a-half-old child. Wastebaskets, dresser drawers, and kitchen cupboards are "grist to his mill." But the observant adult can see that the child's efforts are becoming less random and that he is developing his own style of approaching new problems and situations.

Helping him direct this almost unceasing exploration into occasionally more focused activity becomes a new challenge for the adult. It's especially important to show your interest by sitting down with him for a few minutes and giving him your entire attention as a way of supporting his greater concentration.

Now he wants to imitate a lot of things he sees happening around the house, so make your movements a little more deliberate when you see him watching. This will allow him to observe each step of the process more carefully and imitate it more exactly. Finger-play songs and games at this point give you a chance to teach imitation and at the same time introduce him to the world of make-believe.

Checklist: 18-24 Months
(Developmental Age)

NEW BEHAVIORS	SUGGESTED GAMES	NEW BEHAVIORS	SUGGESTED GAMES
☐ Gestures for communication		☐ Changes from straight line to scribble if asked	63
☐ Attempts to follow directions	53	☐ Walks sideways and backwards	64
☐ Voluntarily relaxes from activities for quiet period	54	☐ Pulls on person to show something	
☐ Tantrums if things go wrong		☐ Uses at least fifteen different words in the right way	
☐ Puts two or more words together to form sentences	55	☐ Matches and compares familiar objects by color	65
☐ Uses signs or words to make wants known	56	☐ Uses some objects in more than one way	66
☐ Discriminates, chooses, makes simple judgments	57	☐ Shows sense of ownership in people and property ("my" mommy, "my" spoon)	
☐ Indicates awareness of role of objects by using them correctly	58	☐ Goes upstairs taking one stair with each foot	
☐ Hands object to adult and awaits reaction	59	☐ Recognizes general family name categories (baby, grandmother, etc.)	67
☐ Seems interested in exploring new places (a friend's house or places in his own home)	60	☐ Makes attempts to replace doll head if removed from doll	68
☐ Extends investigations to wider range of objects	61	☐ Recognizes self in a photograph	69
☐ Washes and dries own hands	62		

119

53. Building Together

HOW ADULT: As the adult plays *blocks* with the child, she collects two groups of three or four blocks, each group with the same shapes as the other. She invites the child to make a train with her. She sets a block in a special place and asks the child to put the like one from his pile right next to it. They continue, with the child placing blocks in the same way as the adult. They talk about "our" train, the adult pointing out they have built it together. She might touch each of the blocks that the child has placed in the line to show him again his part in the building of it. □ To allow the child to be the leader in his turn, the adult lets him remove the blocks in whatever order he chooses. She asks him to decide which block he wants to put away first and she will do what he does. As he removes his block from the train, she says something like, "You're taking the tall one first. Okay, I'll take the other tall one. What are you going to choose for your next one?" □ If they're still having fun, they might want to build another thing together. A similar game may be played another time by stacking the blocks for a tower, stringing a necklace, or building a "fence" with sticks.

CHILD: At first the child may put the block down anywhere because he cannot visualize the finished row. As the line forms, he can begin to see that they're making a row and to understand that his block is helping to make the train. He will enjoy pushing it and making train noises for a few minutes after all the blocks are lined up. □ When it's his turn to be the leader and remove the blocks, the child probably won't pick up in the order they were put down. That doesn't make any difference; it's the opportunity to decide that's important. He enjoys the game even more if he can move around a bit as he plays. Removing the blocks by dropping them off the table into a box adds excitement.

WHY GOAL: To cooperate with the child and let him learn cooperation by building something together. To create a pleasant social experience.

USES: Imitation can provide a rudimentary method for cooperation. When the child has the opportunity to play both roles, the leader as well as the follower, he begins to understand what working together is about.

53. Building Together

HOW Form a partnership with your child and build a block "train." Take turns with him laying down blocks in a line. Talk about how you did it together. Show him that you like to cooperate. Let him play with the train a while before you build the next thing together.

WHY To teach the child a little about cooperation by building something together

54. Cardboard Boxes

HOW Adult: A collection of *sturdy cardboard boxes* is a real treasure in a household with a toddler. The adult gives the child several sturdy cardboard boxes in a place where he has plenty of room to play with them. If the sides are too tall for him to step over, she first lays the boxes on their sides. When he gets into a big box but can't get out, she gently tips it over so he can crawl out. □ She talks to him occasionally about "in," "under," "on," and "out" in order to give him words for what's happening. When the boxes get broken, she gets others. (The adults might begin to bring their groceries home in a box instead of a bag. When the packages are set out the child can play happily with the box while the adult stores the groceries.) □ The adult's role is chiefly that of observer and aide, but she'll have a lot of fun watching his antics. When another child visits, the two will have fun with the boxes, but the adult may need to watch even more carefully.

Child: The child may begin by just sitting and watching the world. Or he may wear a small box on his head and walk around bumping into things and feeling he's hidden to the world. He will learn to get out of a large box by tipping it and rolling out. When he stands on the side of a box, it will probably collapse and he's likely to be startled but not hurt. He may even discover that the bent side makes a good slide. He'll find some things to do that no one else has thought of. □ When he's playing alone, he may like to spend a lot of time just sitting in the box—perhaps with a favorite toy. He feels safe and comfortable in this little house that is totally his. He may even pull the lid down so it's dark and cozy, but he'll want a little peephole to see the rest of the world and to hear someone moving about just to know they're still there. If he has a friend to play with he'll probably be much more active.

WHY Goal: To provide a chance for the child to plan his own play and to have a quiet spot in the bigger world.

Uses: Our organized lives are better balanced if each of us has some time to do as he chooses and some time to be alone.

54. Cardboard Boxes

HOW Playing with cardboard boxes gives the child the opportunity to choose his own kind of play. Sometimes he'll sit cozy and quiet inside his own little "house." Other times he'll want to jump and climb and tumble with the boxes. Give him different sizes and watch how clever he is at thinking up things to do with them.

WHY To give the child a chance to plan his own play and create new games

55. Teaching Words

HOW Adult: You can make a game of being very specific when telling a child the names of objects and actions. That is, instead of saying, "Bring your things, please," say, "Please bring me your shoes and socks." And then to give him a little more verbal help, "I see you brought your blue shoes." ☐ It may take a little more conscious effort at first to label actions. Again, be specific, telling the child not only what you expect him to do but what he is doing or has just done. Instead of "Let's go," use words that help him to know exactly what you mean: "Let's take a ride in the car." Let your praise tell him exactly what he did that you approve of. Saying "good boy" is okay, but it doesn't go far enough. Something like, "You are sitting nicely in your car seat. I'm proud of you," tells him what you feel about his actions and why. ☐ In conversations with the child repeat his own words back to him in simple sentences to give him a pattern for the next time. When he says, "Flower," try to understand what he meant and say back to him, "Yes, it's a pretty flower." Or perhaps what he meant was "I watered the flower." You'll make mistakes, but you'll be right more often than not.

Child: It will be easier for the toddler to know what to do if he hears clearly the names of actions and things. Just talk is not enough. The words he hears must have a relationship to what he's doing. If he has to sort out the information he needs from a long string of words, he is less likely to understand. ☐ He will also learn to say words more quickly if he hears the words at the same time he's performing the action. He then has two clues. When he begins saying the words, he'll just say "water" or "pour water" and depend on the adult to understand.

WHY Goal: To be specific with your language so the child will hear and understand words for objects and actions.

Uses: When it is clear to him what specific words mean, it is only a short step for him to begin saying them.

55. Teaching Words

HOW Help the child learn that words talk to him. Tell him what things are. "This is mommy's flower." Tell him what he's doing. "You're showing Bear the other cars." Tell him how you feel. "I'm glad you're riding with me."

WHY To let the child hear clear words for objects and actions so he will understand

56. Expressing Her Needs

HOW ADULT: While you're helping the child talk about all the new things and happenings in her world, help her also to learn words about herself and her needs. You can show her she has needs by saying:

> You need a spoon for your cereal. I'll get it for you.
> You need a bath before bedtime. Can you find your rubber boat?
> You need a warm coat to go out today. It's chilly outside..

You can encourage her to talk about her own needs by asking:

> What do you need to dig with? Do you have something to put your sand in?
> That's a pretty high shelf. How can you reach it?
> Would it make you feel better if I held you awhile?

CHILD: The child will begin to understand she needs certain things in certain situations. She will be able to answer only in simple words, but she's beginning to think about what she needs. Her emotional needs will probably be harder for her to see, but she may understand a little when they are expressed to her. She will soon express simple, obvious things with words like "hungry" or "cold" or "tired."

WHY GOAL: To learn as a parent to identify, through observation, the child's needs. To give the child words for expressing her needs.

USES: The child begins to see some of her own needs as the adult assists her. She must have words to clearly express needs so they can be met.

56. Expressing Her Needs

HOW Talk to your child about what she needs. "You seem hungry. I think you need something to eat." Ask her questions that help her to say what she needs. "What do you need to dig in the sand?" She will begin one word at a time to express her needs to you. And she'll trust you to work at understanding her.

WHY To give the child words about needs, which she will give back someday soon

57. Sorting with Shapes

HOW ADULT: You can create a sorting game that will involve both judging with the eyes and manipulating with the hands. Give the child a container (such as a *plastic milk jug*) and several *balls* that just fit through the opening. At first, it will be enough simply to put them in, listen for the "clunk," and dump them out. When his interest in this begins to lag, mix some objects such as *blocks* in with the balls. These won't fit through the mouth of the bottle, so they give you an opportunity to say, "That one goes in. Oops, that one doesn't!" □ At this point move on to two *containers* that you have prepared—each having a different-shaped hole. You might say something like, "Good! That ball went in the round hole . . . and now you're putting the block in the square hole." To make sure each object fits in only one hole, try them first in holes you've cut in paper in order to get the right size before cutting the hole in the plastic lid. □ A nice part of this game is that it can continue for months or even several years as you add more shapes and containers. Sorting tasks that offer a great many shapes right from the beginning are likely to be frustrating for the very young child. So if you decide to buy a sorting box, look for one that will allow you gradually to increase the difficulty of the play as the child's skills increase.

CHILD: Most children love putting things in and taking them out, and at first that's all that will happen. But even the one-year-old enjoys learning to sort when he's given just one or two shapes at first. As in other games, the child depends on the adult to provide the right level of difficulty.

WHY GOAL: To provide a manipulative experience through which the child will increase his awareness of shapes and his ability to sort and classify them.

USES: As the child grows older, he can begin to think of the physical world in terms of basic geometric shapes. The direct, manipulative experiences of early childhood are the foundation.

57. Sorting with Shapes

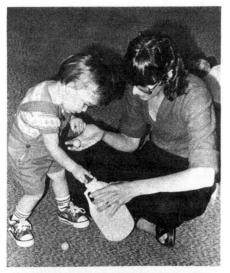

HOW Let the child sort things out by seeing if they will go through a hole. Start by giving him some balls that will just go through the mouth of a plastic milk jug. He'll have fun hearing the balls drop in. Dumping them out is exciting too. Later, show him some blocks and balls to sort into two containers. When he does this well, see what new ideas you can add to the sorting game.

WHY To let the child handle shapes as a way of knowing them well and learning their differences

58. Choices with Lids

HOW ADULT: The adult shows the toddler a *plastic bottle with a screw lid*, shows the child how it "turns," and drops a *little toy* in the bottle. He screws the lid on lightly and gives the jar to the child. If she doesn't try to get the toy, he encourages her to. If she tries to pull the top off, he places his hand on the lid and lets the child put her hand over his so she can feel the turning movement as he takes off the lid. He can do the same thing to show the child how to replace the lid. He lets her play with the jar and some small toys. □ The next time he might give her several small containers with various kinds of lids: a small box with a lid that pushes on, screw-lid jars of several sizes, etc. (In some the adult has put a small toy.) He gives her other things, like large buttons, that will go into the containers. He observes as she tries the lids and moves the objects from one container to the next. He makes suggestions as she needs them for handling the things, but he lets her make the decisions about what goes where.

CHILD: Probably the child will at first lay the screw lid on and try to jam it down. She will turn her hand back and forth, learning only with practice to remove her hand and replace it for the next turn. At first the lids will be crooked, but her skill will improve. Her choices of objects may seem haphazard and no doubt often are, but close observation may show she sometimes follows a self-determined pattern.

WHY GOAL: To give the child practice in turning lids and to provide her with the chance to make choices.

USES: The trial-and-error approach to the solving of a problem is an early step in the thinking process. The child begins to build up a kind of primitive plan for solving a problem through repetition.

58. Choices with Lids

HOW Put a toy inside a plastic jar. (Later she might think it fun if you put her snack inside.) See if your baby will try to take off the lid to get the toy. When she's learned to screw the lid off, give her several things with different kinds of lids. Put some little toys · in them. She can decide which lid to put on and what she wants in each box or jar.

WHY To give the child practice in turning lids and choosing

59. Giving Freely

HOW ADULT: Help your child see that sharing is giving freely, not just of "things" but of trust and feelings and activities. Share yourself by being physically near when she plays. Offer to let her park her small car on your knee or let her hide her block in your pocket. This shows you share her interest in her game. Share your interest in her toy, first by asking to see it and then touching it while she still holds it. If she gives it to you, take it and thank her but return it after a second—before she feels it's lost to her. She will be learning that sharing may mean giving up something only temporarily. □ Play some little games that make it special for her to give. Show her two apples. Tell her one is for her and one is for Joe. Ask if she'd like to give Joe his apple. Label them: "This is Joe's apple and this is yours." She will know exactly what's expected of her (and she'll be certain that her own need to have one will be satisfied). Give her a hug and thank her for giving Joe his apple. Let her see that you value her giving by planning situations for her that make it pleasant to give. She's not yet of age to share in the "dividing" sense of the word, but she's learning from her parents and teachers whom she trusts that giving is a part of loving.

CHILD: The toddler does not know how to take turns, divide things, or give away things she wants. She can be made to give her toy away, but all she will learn is obedience and perhaps resentment. She will usually be quite glad to give when she gives by choice and often will do it quite generously. Don't worry if on the next occasion she's quite selfish. Consistency can't be expected for many years yet.

WHY GOAL: To make giving a pleasant experience and to encourage the natural generosity of the child.

USES: Sharing and giving of feelings provide the child with methods and incentive for the later sharing of ideas and materials.

59. Giving Freely

HOW Let your child share in her own way. She'll show you something that makes her happy. She'll point to exciting things she'd like you to see, too. She'll share her play by letting you hold her baby or stack a block. You can show her you think she's doing a good thing by accepting what she so freely gives.

WHY To make giving a pleasant experience now so it will continue to grow

60. Going Outdoors

Some ideas for your
outdoor language are given
with each photograph.

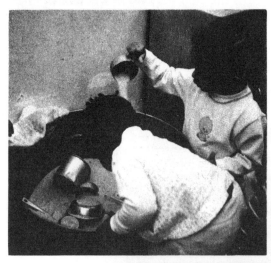

"tastes gritty"
"pour"
"grains"
"trickle down"
"sieve to sift"
"scoop"
"between my fingers"
"dig deep"
"smooth pebble"

"blow"
"warm sun"
"prickly bush"
"soft and silky"
"cool grass"
"smells minty"

60. Going Outdoors

HOW Go with your child and enjoy the outdoors. Let him wander in a safe place. You'll be surprised how many things he finds. Show that you're excited too about the rough rock or shiny leaf he finds. Sing with him as you push his swing. Join him at the sandbox to talk with him about what he's discovering.

WHY To use your language to enrich experiences outdoors

"down deep"
"clunk"
"space between"
"how far down?"
"strong bars"
"cool draft"

61. How Does It Feel?

HOW ADULT: Put in a box *three or four objects* that are quite different to the touch. Let the child open the box and feel the objects. As she handles them, talk about how they feel, using such words as "soft," "rough," "smooth," "heavy," "prickly," etc. Always use the same word to describe the same texture. After a few games remove an object of a certain texture and replace it with another that feels the same. This helps the child understand that "rough" describes the way it feels, not what it is. □ Later put in a *bag* two of the objects that the child has played with, such as a ball and cup. Hold the bag so the child can reach in but cannot see in. Ask her to reach in and find the ball with her fingers. If she brings out the ball, clap or give her a hug and let her play with the ball. If she brings out the other object, say, "That's the cup. It has a handle. Let's put it back and find the ball." Give her clues like, "The ball is round and smooth. Do you remember how it feels when you throw it?" □ Repeat the game using the same objects until the child can choose correctly. Next time add a new object. Eventually use three or four at a time.

CHILD: The child enjoys handling different textures. She may choose one that she likes most or avoid one that is prickly or different from things she usually touches. She'll pick up the adult's attitude about new experiences. □ When she plays the bag game, she may begin by trying to use her eyes to find the ball. Encouraged by such language as, "Find it with your fingers; touch it; find something round," she'll feel for it. When she gets it right several times, she's probably choosing intentionally. She might begin to clap for herself when she brings out the right one.

WHY GOAL: To help the child "see" with her fingers and learn words about what she's touching. To give practice in carrying out verbal requests.

USES: When the child learns words for the feel of various things, she has a new tool for understanding. The child's awareness of tactile differences heightens her enjoyment of such experiences as sand and water play.

61. How Does It Feel?

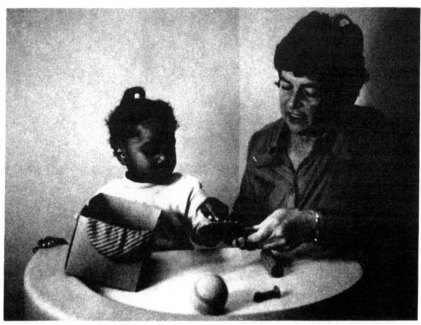

HOW Let the child feel things like a brush, silky cloth, or a cup. Use words that will tell her how they feel—soft, prickly, smooth. Put two in a bag and let her choose the one you name. Have her find it by touching, not looking. Hug her when she gets the right one and let her play with it.

WHY To give the child practice in listening for words that tell her hands what to do

62. Letting Him Paint with Water

HOW ADULT: Find a place where the child can "paint" with water and where you won't have to keep saying "no" to him. Show him how to dip the *sponge* in the *water* and squeeze before he begins to paint. A little water, rather than a bucketful, leaves room for him to squeeze the sponge inside the bucket. □ Point out the shiny wet surface he's painted. Your part is to provide a place and to be sure he's dressed appropriately so you won't have to stop him after he's started . . . and, of course, to let him know he's doing a great job. □ This is a good play activity for out of doors, where porches, steps, tree trunks, and rocks provide good surfaces and water can't hurt anything. If you're painting indoors, put him in a play pen with a sponge and let him "paint" the pen and some toys with water and an old brush. When he has a friend in let them paint together—but with two sponges!

CHILD: The child will begin by watching the surface he's painting. He'll pay no attention to drips—and he'll drip a lot. He doesn't need colored water because the water will make the wood or wall look different and that's what he notices. He'll need to be free to choose what he wants to paint. □ As he becomes more skilled at handling the sponge he may begin to try different arm movements, making more sweeping strokes. And he'll probably become more interested in the sponge, squeezing it and redipping to watch what happens. □ When he's playing with a friend, he'll learn some new ways as he watches and imitates.

WHY GOAL: To allow the child to direct his own play: to help the child play along with another child.

USES: For the very young child each new activity provides many opportunities for decision making and creativity. Self-directed play helps the child develop the self-confidence that will make him comfortable in parallel play, an activity that precedes cooperation.

62. Letting Him Paint with Water

HOW A sponge and a little water in a sand bucket are all that's needed for the child to "paint." Show him how to wet the sponge and squeeze the water out. Take him outdoors or to a room that water can't hurt and let him paint. He'll make a mess, but he'll have great fun finding places to paint and seeing what he can "change" with his paint.

WHY To encourage the child to direct his own play as a way of understanding his own abilities

63. Scribbling

HOW ADULT: Sit with the child at a table with *crayons* and *big paper* for each of you. It usually helps to have the paper taped down. As the child begins to make lines, talk about them—"That's a long, straight line. I'd like to make one like you did." □ Encourage him to notice the way his arm moves so he can feel what it's like when he makes a circle. When he draws spirals, talk about how his arm goes around and around. You can imitate the line on your own paper in order to emphasize a new movement he's discovered. You'll notice the child is making some smaller, more controlled lines. Respond to these changes with such language as "You put that line just where you wanted it." When you've shown some interest, leave him to explore alone. He'll want you to see what he's done later, and you can share more with him then.

CHILD: The child is still just making strokes, and his marks are scribbles, not drawings of things. He's learning to control the marks more and so is beginning to repeat his own lines. Before, he could only see what happened accidentally; now he's trying to make the same thing happen more than once. When he discovers a new way, such as pecking at the paper with the end of the crayon, he'll do just that until he's satisfied. He won't want to stay at the table and work a long time, but he'll like having the things left there to go to when he's in the mood.

WHY GOAL: To help the child notice differences and learn some words for them. To give the child a chance to learn control as he repeats his marks over and over on one occasion and varies them on another.

USES: Practice, or the repetition of an action, is a basic method of establishing fine motor control. The freedom to determine which actions are to be practiced keeps the child moving toward creativity rather than conformity.

63. Scribbling

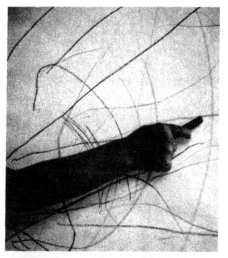

HOW Let your baby know how important you think his scribbles are. Talk about how he made them. "Your arm went round and round." Tell him what he made. "You made a really long line." Talk about how he may feel. "I think you're proud of those marks."

WHY To help the child learn control so he can either repeat or vary his marks as he wishes

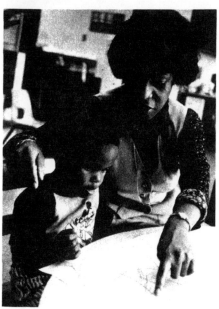

64. Trying New Motions

HOW A<small>DULT</small>: Several new physical skills are beginning to be possible for the toddler. As you walk or play with her, show her some of them. Walk a few steps backward when she's really watching you and say, "I'm walking backward. Can you walk backward?" Help her by walking beside her. □ Another time walk sideways, or on your hands and knees. Make a bridge from a wide board and two bricks. Help the child stand on one end, then go to the other end and encourage her to walk to you. Give her a big hug when she gets there. Walk with her so she'll know you're having fun, too. Try some new jumping games, jumping with both feet. Sing songs about jumping, and as you say the word "jump," jump up with both feet together. □ Some rhymes that could be used are:

All around the chicken coop	1,2,3,4,5
The monkey chased the weasel	I caught a fish alive
That's the way the money goes,	6,7,8,9,10
Jump goes the weasel	He jumped out of my hand

C<small>HILD</small>: The child has just gotten her bearing for walking, so walking backward is a bit difficult. She'll be a little stumbly at first, but she loves the game. Crawling on all fours gives her a refreshing view of the way her world once was. On the bridge she may be a little cautious, but before long she'll probably be running across, and jumping off. The braver children will discover how to stop in the middle and "bounce" the board for a little extra thrill. Later she will like climbing and walking it alone when it is left for her to use.

WHY G<small>OAL</small>: To demonstrate and encourage new ways of moving through space.

U<small>SES</small>: As the child learns that she can do new things with her body successfully, she will be ready to try other new things, such as trike riding or swinging.

64. Trying New Motions

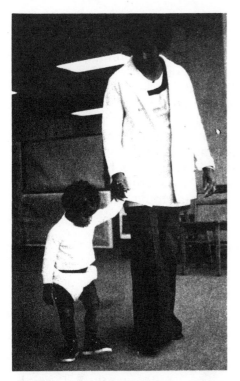

HOW When your child's steady on her feet, move some new ways with her. Walk backward. Build a bridge for her to run across or maybe to bounce on. Jump with both feet off the floor. If you sing about what you're doing, you both have extra fun and she learns the words for the way she's moving.

WHY To encourage new ways of moving and so extend the child's confidence

65. Matching and Grouping Colors

HOW ADULT: When playing blocks with the child, talk about colors, find *three blocks with two of the same color*. (You could also use three colored plastic spoons, three colored toothbrushes, or three colored socks.) Use the words "like" and "same." Show a block in one hand and ask the child, "Can you get the one that's the same color as this one?" If she chooses the wrong color, say gently, "This is yellow. It's not the same," and quietly put it back. If she chooses correctly, praise her. "Great, you found the one that's the same! You found the red block." If she has difficulty, hold the block directly over the matching one or tap it with your block to help her decide. □ Move the blocks around as you play so she chooses by color, not position. More blocks of the same colors may be used after the child becomes skillful at choosing the correct color. Place a red one on a *tray* and a yellow one on *another tray* to provide clues. Encourage her to group blocks on the trays by color. By staying with her and showing pleasure at her efforts, you are letting the baby know she's doing something important.

CHILD: The child may choose either color at the beginning. When she accidentally chooses the "same" and is praised for it, she is more likely to try again. Eventually, she may become the leader in the game—asking the adult to choose. She may vary the game by stacking or putting all of one color in the adult's pocket and enjoy it even more.

WHY GOAL: To help the child know that colors have names. To let the child match items of identical color and learn that things can be grouped by color.

USES: The child can understand and remember a thing better if she can place it in a category such as a color category.

65. Matching and Grouping Colors

HOW Find three common objects (such as toothbrushes) with two of the same color. Pick up one and ask the child, "Can you get the one that's the same color?" If she chooses correctly, praise her. "Great, you found the one that is the same." Later, give her a larger number of the objects to put in two groups.

WHY To show that colors have names and that things can be grouped together by color

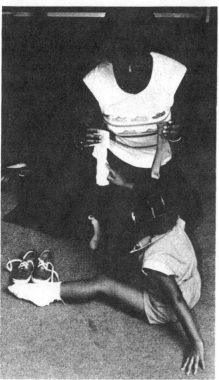

66. Providing Tools

HOW ADULT: When the child's ball rolls just out of his reach under the chair, the adult can help him get it—not by picking it up for him but by giving him a tool to reach it. She can give him his *toy broom* or a *yardstick* and let him reach with that. □ She can set up some situations to show him how useful tools can be as he tries all kinds of new things. When she is setting his *peg board* out for him, she puts the pegs just out of his reach on the table and places a large *wooden spoon* within his reach. If he does not think of using the spoon, she asks if he can get the pegs with the spoon. □ She shows him other tools to use, such as a *stool* to help him reach those places he's not tall enough to reach. (This means the adult will have to take care that she doesn't leave things out that she doesn't want him to reach.) □ When the child is trotting around picking up his toys or just collecting things, as he often does, the adult can show him how to use his *wagon* to move a number of them at one time. If he doesn't have a wagon, she can make one by knotting a cord through a hole low in the end of a cardboard box. The observant adult takes some cues from the child because he's now beginning spontaneously to make tools out of some of his playthings.

CHILD: The child will think this is just a game, but he will be learning that tools can help him to do things he could not otherwise do. When he does such things as using a block to pound with, he's beginning to understand that an object can be used in more than one way. He needs direction in what are appropriate uses of an object. □ Having a stool where he can get it will make him more independent in getting his own toys . . . and sometimes things he shouldn't! That's a part of exploring, too.

WHY GOAL: To show the child how to use a tool to help get something out of reach. To help the child think of new ways to solve a problem.

USES: Being able to solve simple problems using tools leads to more independent and creative behavior.

66. Providing Tools

HOW Help your child use "tools" to do more things for himself. When he can't reach high enough, show him how a stool will help. When his car is too far under the chair, give him a stick and let him poke it out. You'll be pleased to find he's discovering other ways to use things as tools.

WHY To encourage the child to think of new ways of solving a problem

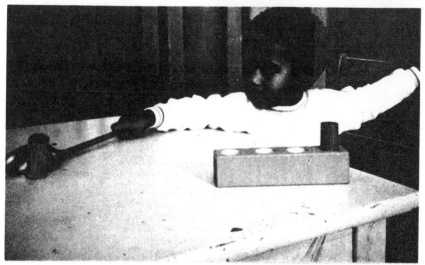

67. Finding Symbols for the Family

HOW ADULT: Talk to your child about families. At the dinner table, or when the family's playing together, talk about how you're a family and name the people there. Or when you're standing close, hug into one big family group. She already has a sense of belonging, but you can give her the words to define the relationship. ☐ Play a game with shapes to help her express her belonging even before she can do it with words. Sit with her and show her a *box of paper shapes* of various sizes and colors (or use some blocks or even spoons of various sizes). Talk about making the family and encourage her to choose a shape to symbolize members of the family. If she can't say all the names, you can do it, but let her say them if she can. Touch shapes she's chosen and name them over to help her remember who's not chosen—and don't forget her. ☐ You might introduce some action by picking up the father shape (or object) and saying, "Daddy's going to buy groceries. Who would like to go with him?" Another time add a big circle or square and say, "This is our house. Who shall we put in the house?" (Avoid making judgments on her choices or trying to read much meaning into the shapes she chooses or the way she places them.) This is a time for a relaxed awareness of the family as a group of people together.

CHILD: The child will enjoy just choosing the shapes and colors. As she hears the words, she will begin to understand the shapes as representing the people and still later understand the relationships. After some time she may begin to show a better understanding by choosing a large shape for a grown-up and a small one for herself. On the other hand, a large shape for herself may simply express "I'm important."

WHY GOAL: To help the child symbolize what her family is and to learn words that define its members.

USES: Naming the family members and seeing the symbolic group helps the child to begin to sort out relationships between people in much the same way she's been discovering physical relationships between objects.

67. Finding Symbols for the Family

HOW Play a "family" game with your child. Give her a box of different-shaped things. Talk about her family one by one. Encourage her to choose a shape for each of the people—and herself. The things you say can add to the comfortable and loving feelings she has for her family.

WHY To give the child some things that will help her think about her family

68. Showing One Part

HOW ADULT: When the adult is playing with the child, he can show her several objects that she knows. He chooses things that look quite different such as a *doll, toy car* and *music box*. Without her seeing, he hides two of them under a *cloth* with only a small special part showing—the feet of the doll, a wheel of the car or the handle of the music box. He asks the child to find the car. If she doesn't recognize it, he moves the toys to a new position and lets a little more of the car show. He continues until she can choose the car dependably. □ Later the adult hides more of the car until the child can recognize it when only a small part is showing. He repeats with other toys, always rewarding with a hug and smile when the child finds it. □ He can use new toys for the next game time, and to make it a richer learning experience, he begins to add more language. As the child chooses the object, the adult can ask her to name it before she takes it from its hiding place. When she answers with an attempt at the right word, the adult responds by telling her, "Yes, it's a car. It has wheels." He lets her have it to play with a minute before going on to the next toy. When the adult makes a big thing of the child's naming the toy, she will enjoy this part of the game as an extra chance to do something that's valued.

CHILD: The child may know some objects right away. She'll be more interested if the adult gives her at least one object that she knows well. Then finding the remaining object is easy and makes her have a good feeling about the game. When the naming rule is added, her words will not always be clear, but we hope she'll try. Hearing the adult's naming helps and she likes having rules if they're simple and reasonable. If she's not ready for this part of the game, it can be used at a later time.

WHY GOAL: To help the child recognize a familiar thing when only part of it can be seen and to say its name.

USES: Recognizing an object when seeing only part of it involves some memory of the object and an important process called visual closure. Learning the word for it means she can begin to express what she knows.

68. Showing One Part

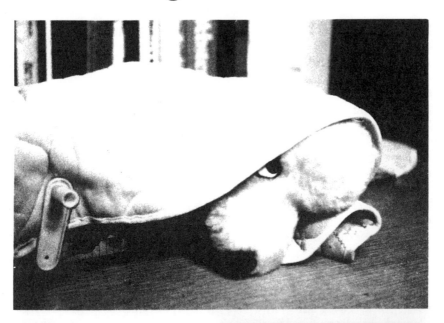

HOW Hide two of your child's favorite toys under a cloth. Leave a part of each toy showing. Ask the child for one of the toys. "Can you find the music box?" See if she can find it by the little part she sees. Uncover it a little more if she needs help and ask again. Later you can add more things. When she can say their names, she may want to hide and let you find.

WHY To help the child recognize a thing when only a part can be seen

69. Making Faces

HOW ADULT: From paper make a *large circle* and a lot of *little circles or shapes* and give them to the child. Point to the big circle and say, "This could be like your face, but what would it need to see with?" If the child doesn't use a little circle to give it an eye, you can suggest it. Ask what else the face needs to be able to eat. Direct the child to thinking about what's needed rather than telling her. □ Talk to the child about her own face and give her a mirror to remind her of what her face looks like. Point out that the eyes are above the mouth, or the nose is in the middle, etc., but don't change what the child has done to make it "prettier." □ Draw faces with *finger paints* or in the *sand* or punch them in *play dough*. Don't confuse her with eyebrows and eyelashes and all that, she'll get around to these when she's ready, probably much later. You're concerned basically with having her understand that this represents a face, so keep it simple.

CHILD: The child may put the small circles anyplace on the large circle at first. But as she begins to see it as a face, she'll start putting the two eyes together and the mouth beneath it. She will be pleased with herself for making something and call it a face or "my face" even if it looks a little odd. She's becoming more aware of herself by making the representation. In her own time she will begin to know that it also needs a nose, ears, and hair as she is able to recall that she herself has them. Perhaps she will ask you for these parts.

WHY GOAL: To teach the child the idea of representation as it relates to herself.

USES: The child will need to know that pictures can tell her about things that are not immediately present. Helping to make a face representation strengthens her self-image.

69. Making Faces

HOW Make a big paper circle like a face. Give the child some little circles and let her add the eyes and mouth. As she learns about noses and ears, she'll want to put them on, too. You're helping her to know more about herself by helping her notice what's needed.

WHY To create a likeness that can strengthen her self-image

24-30 Months

Discovering so many new things and coping with many new feelings makes this an exciting but sometimes difficult period for both the child and the adult. The adults can often anticipate situations that might become frustrating. Close observations of the signs and signals that are unique to their child will enable them to redirect his behavior before that point is reached. Patience, watchfulness, and a little humor can get the adults through many of these rough spots.

There will still be times when nothing seems to help, when maybe the best response is no response at all. Language gives you both a further dimension in understanding as the child attempts to express his feelings, and you respond and expand his words for him.

Reading is a great pleasure for him, and now that he can listen to "real" stories, you can polish up your dramatic talents and read with real enthusiasm. Letting him fill in some of the words in the story or say a line he knows well—("Somebody's been sitting in *my* chair")—makes the storytelling a partnership in language.

Reverting to "baby" behavior (which sometimes happens) is perhaps the child's way of letting you know he's confused and a little fearful of the present. Respond warmly to his need for "babying." But be sure that your greatest approval comes when he's displaying his "big boy" behavior.

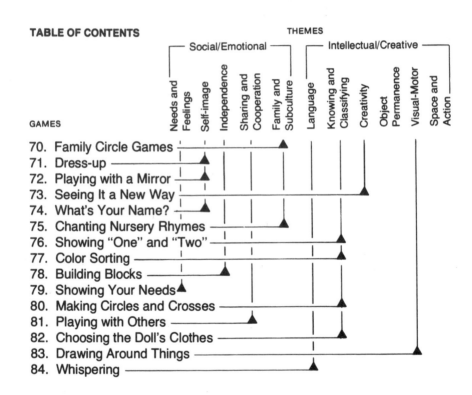
156

Checklist: 24-30 Months
(Developmental Age)

NEW BEHAVIORS	SUGGESTED GAMES	NEW BEHAVIORS	SUGGESTED GAMES
☐ Imitates play of others	70	☐ Understands and uses correctly fifty words	
☐ Listens to simple stories, especially liking those heard before		☐ Uses simple speech equivalent to obtain wants	79
☐ Carries on conversation with self and dolls	71	☐ Shows (by asking or gestures) the need to go to the toilet	
☐ Finds own play area or activity	72	☐ Has enough eye-hand ability to copy a line	80
☐ Explores surroundings in new or modified ways	73	☐ Shows pleasure in dealing with people and things	81
☐ Understands and stays away from common dangers		☐ Likes to "help" parents around the house (raking leaves, setting table)	
☐ Uses size words (large, big, little, small) often and correctly		☐ Usually knows when certain clothes, activities, or toys are appropriate	82
☐ Sometimes gives first and last name when asked	74		
☐ Repeats parts of nursery rhymes or joins in	75	☐ Differentiates circle and square forms	83
☐ Understands the concept of one	76	☐ Takes things apart for the purpose of learning	
☐ Groups things together by color, form, or size	77	☐ Likes to listen (acquires sense of descriptive power of words)	84
☐ Enjoys using comparisons (color, form, size) in self-directed play	78		

70. Family Circle Games

HOW ADULT: Give some of your time to playing family games with your child. Most adults have special memories of games or family activities that were unique to their family. Pass some of these on to your children. These special times and memories may grow out of only a few minutes of being together. Play some circle games with your child, it only takes two to play Ring Around the Rosie, but it's lots more fun if the whole family's playing. □ When you're listening to some music, form a band and all of you play together. You don't need real instruments; pans and spoons are just as much fun, and anybody can play them. Dancing can be fun together. Hold the child in your arms as you dance or be his partner and follow him. You'll work out some funny dances when the whole family's in the act. □ Take your cues from the child sometimes and play the game he invents. Each of you will have a better understanding of the other and will be playing a role in building your family traditions.

CHILD: The child will be learning how to get along in the world as he participates in family activities (either with his family at home or with his day-care family). He'll be willing to try new things because he feels secure in this warm, loving group. He will trust in his own abilities to contribute to a group, since even his clumsiest efforts are applauded and encouraged.

WHY GOAL: To make the family supportive to the child. To give the child practice in being a part of a group.

USES: The child needs progressively to know how to live peacefully with his peers and confidently with outside adults. He is learning the control (in the gentle atmosphere of the family) that he'll need as he begins to expand his social world.

70. Family Circle Games

HOW Plan some special times when the whole family or the day care cluster can play together. Play the child's favorite circle games or dance together. Form a marching band and play on pans with spoons. He'll feel he has an important place in this loving group.

WHY To have fun . . . and let the child feel support from the family

71. Dress-up

HOW ADULT: Provide the child with a box of *simple dress-up things*. Enjoy draping a scarf about yourself or putting on a hat, and then encourage the child to put on some of the things. Show him a *mirror* he might use and talk about daddy's boots or the rain hat, or the bright red tie—then let him decide what to try. □ Try to limit yourself to making positive comments about his choices or to helping him if he asks. Don't get upset if a girl wears her daddy's hat or a boy wears jewelry; we all need to try out various roles to understand what they're like. □ Add new things to the box occasionally and remove some of the old ones, remembering that such simple things as shoes and beads and hats work best.

CHILD: The child may put on only a hat or bracelet or throw a scarf over his head. He likes things he can manage by himself, such as purses or shoes or hats. At this stage he is not interested in "costumes," only in seeing how it feels to be a little different. He does not want the adult to dress him, though he might want a little help with what he's choosing. □ Sometimes he tries on everything, but another time he puts one thing on and wants to wear it all day. No matter if his hat is backward or his shoes big enough to fall off his feet—he'll feel he's a special person, and he will know he can change any time he wants.

WHY GOAL: To provide a chance for the child to decide things for himself and about himself. To help the child feel that growing up is good by dressing up with mother's or daddy's things.

USES: The child who feels good about himself because his decisions have been accepted will have a more positive attitude in his approach to other people. Growing up takes a long time. Having a chance to sample various future roles makes the long wait more productive and more tolerable.

71. Dress-up

HOW Give your child a chance to be someone new and different. Show him a box of simple dress-up things. Leave him alone to decide what he'd like to wear. But let him know you like what he chooses. Laugh and have fun with him, but be careful not to laugh at him.

WHY To give a chance for the child to decide things about himself

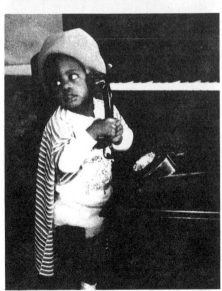

72. Playing with a Mirror

HOW ADULT: The adult gives the child a chance to get to know herself better by occasionally giving her a *hand mirror*. He gives her a *comb* or *toothbrush* or *washcloth* and lets her play with them as she watches what's happening in the mirror. He responds to some of her actions, saying things like "You're washing your nose." "The comb gets caught in your hair, doesn't it?" But mostly he just observes, staying close as long as she has the mirror. □ He can place a big mirror low where the child can see herself and have room to move about. This gives her a chance to see her whole body in action. The adult can join the child and talk about the image as he touches the child, "This is Jenny. Your hands are on your head." He has fun imitating some of her motions but realizes she needs to play the game by herself a lot. A box with hats and scarves or some jewelry, kept near the mirror, provides new fun.

CHILD: The child thinks it's fun to see her image. She'll probably dance around and pose or make faces. It will help her feel important to know she can make the image do whatever she wants it to. Sometimes she may just make a face and walk away. Another time she may enjoy watching herself for some time practicing smiles, sticking out her tongue, or pulling her eyes open . . . examining her face as she would a new doll.

WHY GOAL: To give the child a chance to learn more about herself. To let her see what she feels her body doing.

USES: The more the child learns about herself and what she can do, the more poise she will have in new situations.

72. Playing with a Mirror

HOW Give your child a hand mirror or fasten a mirror down low. You'll get to know more about her as you watch her discovering herself. Give her a comb or toothbrush so she can feel what she sees happening in the mirror. Laugh with her as she tries out new faces.

WHY To let the child see what she feels her body doing

73. Seeing It a New Way

HOW ADULT: In this game a *magnifying glass* is given to the child. When he has examined it and notices that it makes things seem different, the adult talks about "big" and "different." As the child plays alone, the adult tries to respond to his questions and feelings, but she lets the discovery be the child's. The adult's role is to provide the opportunities for using the glass. (Trying to help him see what you think he should see will probably discourage him.) □ The adult takes the glass along when she takes her child for a walk, or sometimes lets him look at his food on the plate before he eats. And she gives him the glass when he goes to the supermarket with her, where he'll have yards and yards of things to see on his own eye level.

CHILD: Once the child understands what the glass will do, he will have great fun observing simple things in a new way. He'll wander from one thing to the next just looking. He'll take the glass away, look at the object, then try it again through the glass. He probably won't be able to understand he's looking at the parts of a flower; he'll just know the flower is no longer the same. He won't even be able to express what he sees, but he'll want to share the excitement of the experience.

WHY GOAL: To provide a nondirected experience through which the child can discover that things do not always look the same.

USES: Seeing familiar things in a new way broadens and enriches the child's concepts. As he remembers the object as it was and adds to that the knowledge of what he's seeing, he uses a basic cognitive process called assimilation.

73. Seeing It a New Way

HOW How many things can your child see with a magnifying glass? Give him one and show him what it does. Let him find things to look at. He'll look at familiar things, but they'll all seem new. Look when he asks you and share his wonder.

WHY To provide a way for the child to see that things do not always look the same

74. What's Your Name?

HOW ADULT: Sometimes when the adult is with her child, she takes a special minute to help him say his name. She makes up little rhymes with his name or sings him songs about himself. She occasionally uses his whole name when she talks to him. □ "Thank you, Bill Green." And she uses the family name when talking to others in the family so he can hear that it's the same for all of them. She makes up activities in which he must tell his name. Perhaps he could knock on the kitchen door, and the adult could ask, "Who is it?" She introduces him to other people by his name. A picture album with his own picture and pictures of his friends and family will help him to see that every person has a name. The adult speaks his name clearly so he can learn it and recognize it when others speak it. (She can save her very special pet name for him for their private times.)

CHILD: At first the child may say only one part of his name. As he hears it spoken clearly, he will begin to learn to say it more clearly and to know that it is his. He'll be delighted to name himself in his pictures, though he may say "me" at first. Some children will use their names for a while when they talk about themselves and later switch to "I" and "me."

WHY GOAL: To give the child practice saying and meaningfully using his two names as a way of strengthening his identity.

USES: It is important to know who you are and what family you belong to. Names help to define that knowledge.

74. What's Your Name?

HOW Say your child's name to him in songs and stories. Use his last name, too. "Thank you, Bill Green." Make up games where he tells his name. Share his delight when he names his own photograph.

WHY To give the child practice saying his two names and so to strengthen his self-image

75. Chanting Nursery Rhymes

HOW ADULT: When the child begins to enjoy trying new words, the adult helps with simple nursery rhymes. They repeat the ones they read together, choosing the shorter ones first. If a rhyme is too long, she uses only a couple of lines. □ The adult speaks clearly so the child can hear all the words. Sometimes she chants the rhyme in a sing-song way; sometimes they act it out. The adult makes sure that the favorite nursery rhymes of the family and cultural group are taught. Older children in the family usually like to do this with "the baby."

Baa Baa, black sheep,	Tengo, Tengo, Tengo
Have you any wool?	Tu nu tienes nada
Yes, Sir. Yes, Sir.	Tengo tres ovejas,
Three bags full.	En mi manada.
One for my master,	Una me de leche,
And one for my dame,	Una me da lana,
And one for the little boy	Y otra mantequilla,
Who lives in the lane.	Para la semana.

CHILD: The child enjoys hearing words, and when they're said with a rhythm or as a part of his bath or of the game he's playing, he enjoys them even more. At first he may yell out just the few words that sound alike, but as the time goes on he'll learn to say them. Many children like acting them out and can do that before they can say the words.

WHY GOAL: To teach the words and rhythm of the language. To help the child learn traditional rhymes.

USES: Using the language and traditions of the group helps the child begin to feel a part of a group.

75. Chanting Nursery Rhymes

HOW You will want to teach the nursery rhymes of your own childhood to your child. You can chant them or sing them or act them out. The child loves to hear them repeated again and again as he learns to say them, too.

WHY To help the child know the rhymes of his cultural group

76. Showing "One" and "Two"

HOW ADULT: Look for occasions when you can talk about "one" and "more than one" with the child. Take some special time to sit with the child and play a game with "one." A number of *things* can be put in stacks on the table or in bowls. Talk to the child about groups: "See this bowl has a lot. This bowl has just a few. This bowl has only one." Ask the child to dump the bowl that has one. Jumble all the things together and ask her to put one in each bowl. Whenever she chooses correctly, give her a hug and tell her, "You chose just one." □ After the child knows "one," look for times to talk about "two." Show the child two *socks*, two *shoes*, or two of us together. Place some stacks of *pennies* on the table, some with two pennies and some with one. Ask the child to put all the stacks that have one penny on a corner and the stacks of two on another. Say the word "two" as you play and be sure to give your special reward when she's correct. □ When the child knows "two," some parents may decide to go on to "three." This game should stretch over many months. A lot of practice is needed.

CHILD: The word "one" may at first mean the name of the object to the child. As she plays the game, she'll understand it's telling how many. "One" will be an easy word for her to learn to say. When playing, she'll find it more fun to handle the objects in some way than to just point. When she plays with two, she may quickly learn to say the word, but for a while "two" may mean anything over one. She loves to be right and practice helps her to know.

WHY GOAL: To strengthen the number concepts of "one" and "two." To help her say the words.

USES: Grouping helps the child see relationships and make primitive comparisons. Learning that one is different from many is a broad initial discrimination that will be followed by many closer discriminations.

76. Showing "One" and "Two"

HOW As you live with your child, use the word "one" to show her how many. Play a special game with her. Show her groups of things that have "one," "two," or "many" in them. Encourage her to pick out the group that is "one." Don't forget the reward she likes best (a pat, a kiss, a clap) whenever she chooses the group of one.

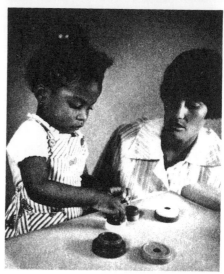

WHY To show that "one" and "two" tell a particular amount

77. Color Sorting

HOW Adult: Color games can be made from many of the color toys the child is now using. When he's beginning to tire of his block play, give the child a number of *trays* and ask him to sort his *blocks* by putting all the red ones on one tray, the blue ones on another tray, etc. Don't give him cues by putting a block on each plate unless he really needs you to. Instead, if he has trouble starting, ask him some questions such as, "What color are you going to put here?" "Which blocks go on this plate?" Let him make the decisions. Praise him by telling him what he has done; "Good, you put that green block with the other green ones." Smile and laugh to let him know he's done a good thing. □ Play a color game sometimes when he's using his *peg board*. (Be sure the pegs are in a tray so he can think about the game and not be chasing the pegs.) Put all the red pegs in a row or make a frame of one color and an inside square of another. Let him decide the pattern when he can. Ask questions that help him tell you about it, such as, "What color did you use on the top?" Perhaps a rule of the game might be to say the color as the peg is picked up or put into the hole.

Child: The child knows now how to match colors, and when he understands the rules of the game, he will enjoy playing with the adult, making more decisions, and having a larger number of objects to choose from. But it may not be until the kindergarten year that the child can correctly name and choose all the colors.

WHY Goal: To give the child experience in saying color words and in sorting many items by color categories.

Uses: Knowing the color names will enable the child to express himself more adequately. We do not expect him to do it perfectly now, but he deserves to have a chance to use the color words he does know and be complimented on these. With opportunities he'll gradually add more color words to his vocabulary.

77. Color Sorting

HOW Give the child a number of trays. (These could be plates or box lids.) Ask him to sort his blocks by putting all the red ones on one tray, the blue ones on another tray, etc. Ask him some questions, such as, "What color are you going to put here?" "Which blocks go on this plate?" Smile and laugh to let him know he's done a good thing. Later, see what kinds of color patterns he can make with some pegs. Encourage him to use the color words as he plays the game.

WHY To give the child experience saying some color words and sorting by colors

78. Building Blocks

HOW A<small>DULT</small>: The adult gives the child a box of *blocks of various sizes and shapes*. She looks at what he has done and talks to him about it: "That is a very high tower." "The purple one you put on top looks pretty." She gives him a chance to talk about what he's done or leaves him alone if he doesn't want to talk. ☐ If the child throws or hits with the blocks, the adult discourages him and shows him how they can be used. She might give the child a fewer number to begin with, but once he's learned what he can do, she wants to make sure that he has enough to be able to make choices. Cans and small cardboard boxes of varying sizes make excellent building blocks. Any blocks that require decisions about balance are better than a collection of blocks of one size and shape. ☐ The adult may find it hard to stay out of the fun, so when she sees he's about ready for a change, she can join him and build for him to knock down.

C<small>HILD</small>: He may not know how to place blocks, at first, but he'll learn more quickly if he is allowed to try his own way. Many young children make long flat lines on the floor before they begin stacking blocks. Perhaps he may stack only two or three, knock them down, and begin again. He may take a very long time to balance one block. It's very discouraging for him to work so hard and then have the structure tumble before he's ready, as it does sometimes. He will want some comfort and understanding then as well as approval when he's successful.

WHY G<small>OAL</small>: To provide a time for him to direct his own actions. To notice how he goes about things and to help him feel good about what he can do.

U<small>SES</small>: The child's self-reliance will increase as he learns that he can successfully accomplish what he tries to do.

78. Building Blocks

HOW How can you play a game with building blocks? By showing you're interested and by giving the child a chance to choose the way he wants to do things. You can show you're interested by talking about what he's done. "You put the purple block right on top." Another time he might want it to be a sharing game. Add cans and small boxes to give him more chance for choices.

WHY To provide a time for him to direct his own actions

79. Showing Your Needs

HOW ADULT: Now that your child is becoming more aware of her needs, help her to see they can be expressed. Do this by expressing some of your needs. Talk in simple terms to your child about what you need, and at the same time give her a reasonable way in which she might help:

> I need to use the phone.
> *You may bring your doll over here to play while I talk.*
> I need to rest a little.
> *Let's find some books for you to read on your bed.*
> I need someone to love me.
> *Do you have a big hug or kiss for me?*
> I need another spoon.
> *Could you get me one from the drawer, please?*

When she has helped, tell her how helpful she was when you really needed her. Sometimes make up a little pretending game that your child might think is funny. Say, "I'm pretending it's raining. What do I need to go outside?" or "Here's my bowl of soup, what do I need to eat it with?"

CHILD: The child will do more than just listen when she's given a chance. She'll feel very proud when the adult praises her. "I needed someone to hold the door. Thank you for doing it."

WHY GOAL: To model words the child can someday use to express her needs. To help her understand that others have needs.

USES: By responding to the need statements of others, the child is moving very gradually toward the important ability to take the viewpoint of others or to empathize.

79. Showing Your Needs

HOW Teach your child how to express her needs by expressing yours. "I need a big spoon." Let her know how to help you with your needs. "Can you get me a spoon?" She will feel good that she can do something for you. But she will also be learning how to talk about what she needs.

WHY To let your child help you so she will know that others have needs

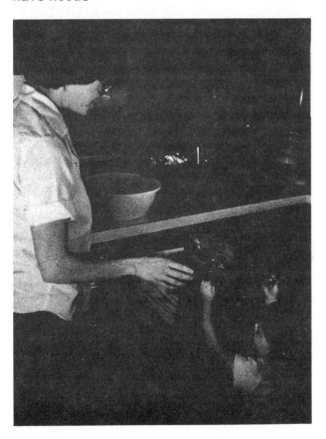

80. Making Circles and Crosses

HOW ADULT: When you have seen the child draw lines that look a little like circles, play some new games with her. Make circles out of *blocks* with the child inside; trace *cup rims* with your fingers; draw big and little circles with *crayons*; with a couple of friends make a circle around a toy; use fingers to form an O; take a straight *rope* and bring the ends to touch and make a circle. Talk about curved lines and closed lines. □ Another time show her how to make a straight line go over another straight line and talk about crosses. See how many games using crosses you and the family can invent as you did with circles. Words to say: circle, cross, closed, line, straight.

CHILD: The child will like making fences around herself with the blocks and rope, though she may have to step out to see it's a circle. (She'll begin to see that lines must be curved and closed to be a circle.) If she draws them, they may be crooked and not quite closed. That's okay, they'll be different from the straight lines and that's the essential thing she's learning. She will need time to understand and say the words that tell her about the differences. She does begin soon to recognize which is a circle and which is a cross.

WHY GOAL: To help the child understand through experience the differences between a circle and a cross; to use words that tell the difference.

USES: Recognizing differences in physical attributes of abstract symbols is another step in learning to classify things. Practice in distinguishing signs and symbols may make a small contribution later to the learning of reading and math.

80. Making Circles and Crosses

HOW Make a circle of blocks or sticks with your child. Let her sit inside so the circle is all around her. Use the word "circle." Think of some ways to let her make crosses. You're helping her to see that something, like a line, can change to be several different things.

WHY To provide a vivid experience that will help her recognize forms

81. Playing with Others

HOW ADULT: Sometimes when two toddlers are playing with a *ball* the adult might show them how to toss the ball with a *blanket*. She lets them each hold two corners of the blanket, and then she drops a light ball in the middle. They'll probably begin to shake the blanket, but if not, the adult says something like, "What can you make the ball do?" □ By telling them what is happening, she can help them see their part in the game. She says things like: "John, you're holding your side up so the ball won't roll off. You can make the ball bounce because you're playing together. Two people are having fun in this game!"

CHILD: The children enjoy making the ball do something. They will think of many ways to bounce it. They will see (at their own level of understanding) that the game goes well when they try to help each other. They learn that the ball won't stay on the blanket unless each one holds his end. They'll drop the ball a lot or bounce it over the side, but chasing it is part of the fun. They will probably invent some other ways to play and may end the game just throwing the ball around.

WHY GOAL: To help the child begin to learn to play cooperatively with another child. To engineer a situation where cooperation is more satisfying than competition or solitary play.

USES: Many human activities (most of the more complex ones) can be accomplished only through cooperative behavior. The child who has had some real enjoyment from early cooperative games is more likely to positively approach later situations involving cooperation.

81. Playing with Others

HOW Two toddlers can be partners in a special kind of ball game. Give each child one end of a small blanket or large towel. Toss a light ball into the middle of the blanket. Let them make the ball bounce by shaking the blanket. There'll be much fun as they learn to depend on each other not to drop the blanket.

WHY To create a situation where cooperation works best

82. Choosing the Doll's Clothes

HOW ADULT: Make a *large paper doll* and some *simple clothes* for it. Invite your child to talk about what clothes the doll might wear. Help her choose clothing by naming the pieces. Ask things like: "What shall we put on his feet? Can you find something for him to wear outside so he will be warm? Tell me something he can put on his head." Let the child choose the shirt or the socks and lay them on the doll. Encourage her to name them as she chooses. □ In this game be interested in the child's learning the words and matching the clothing to the right parts of the body, not with style. Show her some children in a mail-order catalog and talk about what they're wearing. Let her find a child who's ready to play outside, or is dressed for bed, etc. Talk about how you know: "He has his warm winter coat on." □ Later you can ask her to tell you what the picture child is getting ready to do. You'll get some very interesting observations!

CHILD: The child may at first confuse shirts and pants, etc., and put them on the wrong parts of the doll, but she'll soon get them straight and begin to say their names. She pays no attention to which shirt "looks good" with which pants, she's just delighted to be able to choose by herself. □ When she looks at the pictures, she will point and name some of the clothing. She'll begin to choose the proper thing for the weather or the activity when she's guided by the adult's questions.

WHY GOAL: To help the child learn the words for the clothing she needs. To give her a reason for evaluating and choosing.

USES: Talking about clothes in the game will help the child become more aware of her own clothing and encourage her interest in helping to dress herself and making the decisions necessary in dressing.

82. Choosing the Doll's Clothes

HOW Enjoy looking at a catalog together. Let your child learn the words for her clothes as she finds them in the pictures. Give her a paper doll and let her choose the clothes to put on it. She'll have more interest in dressing herself when she can choose for herself and enjoy sharing the words with you.

WHY To give the child a reason for making choices

83. Drawing Around Things

HOW ADULT: When the child learns to hold a *pencil*, she often wants to "write" like the grown-ups do. The adult can make some of her "writing" times more fun by giving her something to draw around. □ He shows her how to hold a box or cup and draw around it with her finger and then with a pencil, crayon, or marker. He follows the lines with his finger and has the child trace them to see that they are like the bottom of the box. If the child doesn't want to try, he lets her use the pencil for "writing" and they trace another day. □ After the first time, they look for things together. Handling an object to decide if it is what they want, tracing its edges, and talking about it makes it much easier to see how it's different from another object. The adult guides the decision toward simple objects with simple outlines to trace (such as *blocks, cups, plates*).

CHILD: The child will like having a chance to use the pencil, but at first she will not be very good at drawing around the object. She may make only a line on one side and then just scribble. When she does begin tracing, her lines may not look much like the outline of the object. □ Finding things herself makes her more aware of the shape, and she'll be more eager to trace when she's helped to choose. As she gradually learns to use the pencil, she follows the shape more closely.

WHY GOAL: To provide a pleasant experience through which the child can practice controlling the small muscles of her hands. To help her see differences in the shapes of objects.

USES: Tracing an object helps the child better understand the relationship of a representation (in this case an outline) to an object. Fine motor control is essential to many later skills including writing. This game may provide a small increment in the long process of bringing the complex muscles of the hands under control.

83. Drawing Around Things

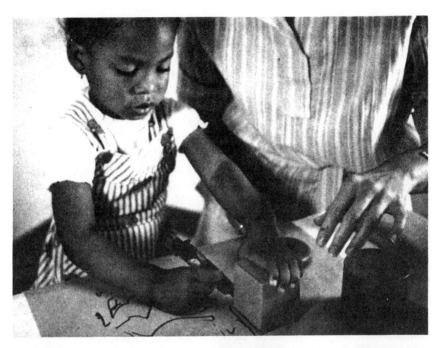

HOW Give the child a plastic cup to draw around. Have her trace the edge of the cup with her finger. Then give her a pencil or marker to use. Talk about the circle she drew. Help her find some other objects with simple shapes to trace. You're helping her use her hands and make pictures of the objects so she'll know more about the ways they're different.

WHY To let her practice using the small muscles of her hands

84. Whispering

HOW Adult: Voices can become tiresome if they always sound the same. Make your voice more interesting to hear by speaking higher or lower or whispering. Whispering's a way to make it special for just you two. It's a way to help her feel close and calm. □ Get the child's attention, make her feel special, show your surprise or delight or displeasure by changing the tone of your voice. You are helping her really to hear what you say by creating a change in your speech pattern. You're using the same words, but you make it novel when you change the tone, and she responds positively to novelty. □ Respond to the child's voice change with expressions that show you really heard or are surprised or whatever else she's trying to convey. If you're used to saying "I love you" in a quiet whispering voice, try a loud, joyous "I love you." Go up to her and whisper when she might expect you to call across the room. Sing your words to help her relax. Use your lowest voice to make her laugh. She'll listen more closely and be much more interested in producing language.

Child: The child is using her voice in many ways—yelling, crooning, and saying a few words. But mostly she's listening and observing. She will be found listening intently to a telephone conversation or to adults talking. Maybe it's the rhythm of the language and the tones of the voices she's learning. □ When she plays whispering games with the adult, she's learning how to control her voice and make it do what she wants it to. Right now it's just a funny way to talk that tickles and makes her laugh. She doesn't consciously imitate the tones right after she hears them, but they'll appear as her use of words increases. Once she gets started, she'll probably have lots of fun whispering to a peer or sibling.

WHY Goal: To vary your voice so that it stays interesting to the child and encourages her to vary hers.

Uses: Language is dependent upon intonation and rhythm as well as words. One word can mean several things, depending on the way it's said: "Yes" (I'm listening), or "Yes" (I agree). The child needs to hear variety in order to create it with her own voice.

84. Whispering

HOW Feed your child's interest in words by changing your voice when you talk. Whisper sometimes. That's tickly, and she will really listen and laugh! Call her by singing her name. Keep her interested in hearing words by changing the way you say them. If she's listening, she's probably learning. Try a loud, joyous "I love you!"

WHY To vary your voice so it stays interesting to the child

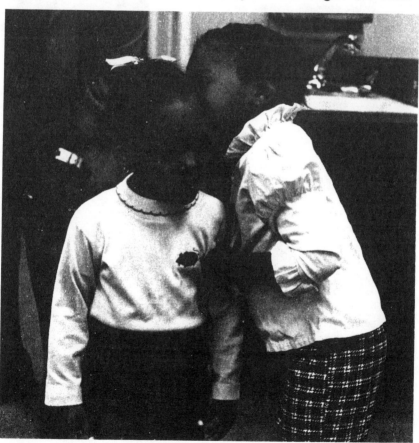

30-36 Months

The period just before the third birthday is characterized by a refinement and extension of skills already acquired. Pretending and imagination grow to include a few short, original stories and the ability to start thinking "what if." Dressing now includes some mastery of snaps, buttons, and zippers. Eating is completed with only occasional accidents, and toileting has become routine for many children.

Language development is progressing too. Words defining space (in, out, up) and time (after, before, next) and word endings (-ed, -ing, -s) are becoming a part of the child's listening and speaking vocabulary. You can encourage the child to use the words he knows by asking wh-questions, questions that begin with *what*, *where*, and *who*. (*Why* and *when* come later.)

"Read" his gestures, but give the child words to help him verbalize what he is trying to share with you. Responding to his language by careful listening and by respecting what he has to say gives him encouragement. It even helps to say, "I like it when you use your voice to tell me." Not everything he says requires a long conversation; sometimes a nod or smile is just right. But these make talking worthwhile by showing him that you're listening.

TABLE OF CONTENTS

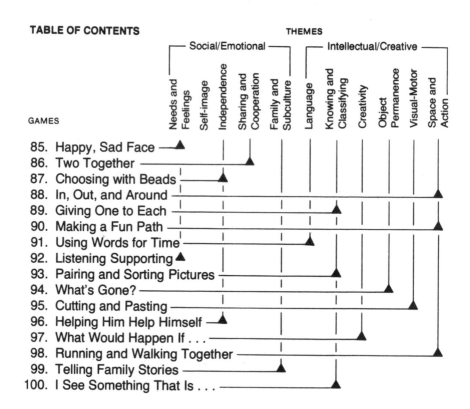

Checklist: 30-36 Months
(Developmental Age)

NEW BEHAVIORS	SUGGESTED GAMES
☐ Uses short sentences to convey simple ideas	85
☐ Understands the idea of waiting for someone else to go first	86
☐ Follows simple rules in group games run by an adult	
☐ Takes apart and puts together purposefully	87
☐ Understands in, out, and under	88
☐ Puts on own coat and shoes (without buttoning or tying)	
☐ Counts two, indicates awareness of "one more"	89
☐ Hops on one foot and walks upstairs and downstairs, placing one foot on each stair	90
☐ Knows that different activities go on during different times of the day	91
☐ Expresses feelings, desires, and problems verbally	92
☐ Compares size; puts size comparison to practical use	93
☐ Remembers and names objects absent for a short time	94
☐ Uses scissors with one hand to cut paper	95
☐ Feeds himself, using a fork and/or spoon and glass in the right way	96
☐ Deals verbally with nonpresent situation	97
☐ Child recognizes picture of an object even when shown a different view	
☐ Runs freely	98
☐ Acts out (singly or with others) simple stories	99
☐ Identifies object by its use	100

85. Happy Face, Sad Face

HOW ADULT: A child can be helped to understand and accept his own feelings better when he knows that not just Mom and Dad but all people have feelings. Show the child *pictures of faces* that clearly show an emotion. Talk about the expressions on the faces. Help him to tell you how he thinks the people feel. See if he can remember something that has made him feel that way—happy or angry or sad. Encourage him to say what he thinks made them sad and what might make them happy. (Avoid "why" questions because these are harder to answer.) □ Talk about the people in the pictures of his favorite story books and let him tell you what they're laughing or crying about. □ Tell him how you feel: "I feel sad. May I tell you about it?" Help him to say how he is feeling: "I see you look angry. Can you tell me what happened?" Sometimes all you can do is comfort him and let him know you love him and you understand his confusion.

CHILD: Seeing feelings expressed on faces around him or in pictures will make it easier for him to learn the words for those feelings. It will take the child a long time to be able to sort out his feelings and to give names to them. He'll still throw, or hit, or jump up and down—because even when he knows some words, he may not know just what kind of feeling he's having right now. He'll need lots of patience and love as he sorts all this out. As he hears other people talk about their feelings, he will begin to see that sometimes he can use words instead of actions.

WHY GOAL: To help the child begin to understand the feelings of others and learn some words for feelings.

USES: Understanding that others have the same feelings he has helps the child begin to broaden his totally personal view of the social world and allows him to imitate more mature ways of expressing feelings.

85. Happy Face, Sad Face

HOW Help your child to sort out his happy and unhappy feelings. Let him see pictures of other people showing their feelings. Give him some words to tell him how they feel: "angry," "happy," "sad." Comfort him with hugs and loving when he's unhappy, and help him use the words to express it. Hug him and love him when he's happy so he will know you like him that way, too.

WHY To help the child notice the feelings of others as a step in understanding his own

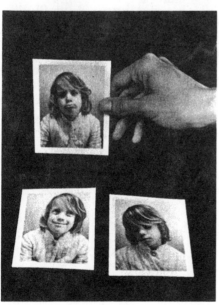

86. Two Together

HOW ADULT: A soft *sponge ball* is a great toy for the toddler. When the adult sees the child trying to kick the ball, he shows her how to kick with her toe instead of the bottom of her foot. When two toddlers are playing together, he gives them each a ball and lets them play side by side. They're not skillful enough to kick the ball back and forth to each other, but they like to play beside someone who's playing the same game. And they may exchange a few kicks of the ball. □ Later, the two can have a little more of a partnership in a simple rolling game. The adult makes a slanted place to roll a big ball down and shows the children how to play together. One child stands at the top and rolls the ball down. The other child picks it up and goes to the top of the board to roll it as the first child goes around to pick it up. The adult encourages each child to play her own part. They'll do it only a couple of turns; then the adult gives them each a ball to roll and starts off with one ball again at the beginning of the next play time. If they invent a new way to use the ball cooperatively, he encourages them, of course! (This game is more open-ended than the cooperative game of bouncing the ball in the blanket, #81, and therefore potentially more demanding.)

CHILD: When the child is learning to kick, she'll simply walk into the ball with a shuffling motion. Gradually she will learn to raise her foot and kick, and when the ball sails, she's delighted. She may try so hard she becomes unbalanced and she finds that's funny, too. □ When she plays with a friend, it's the companionship she enjoys. She's not good at open-handed partnerships yet, but she may give it a try if she's encouraged.

WHY GOAL: To give the child a chance to learn to kick a ball, to learn to play with a peer, and to have an open-ended opportunity for cooperation.

USES: Parallel or side-by-side play is a forerunner of cooperation with another child. Learning cooperation first with parents, then with peers, then with larger groups is a lifetime process—but it can start early if we don't expect it to be perfect.

86. Two Together

HOW Show your child how to kick a ball. When she's playing with a friend, give them each a ball to kick. They may play with the same ball for a minute or two, but mostly they'll play side by side. Tell them you're glad to see them playing well "together." Later, let them roll a ball down a board.

WHY To give the child a chance to play happily with a peer

87. Choosing with Beads

HOW ADULT: Now is the time for the adult and child to begin a collection of objects to put into a bead *box*. They find things with a hole or things which can have a hole punched: colored *paper shapes, shells with holes,* wooden *beads, buttons, macaroni, or pretty bits of cloth.* The adult should add several *strings* or shoe *laces* of various lengths and colors. □ Sometime when the child is dressing up, the adult might get the box and show the child how he can make his own beads to wear. She shows him how to push the end of the string through the big bead. When the bead slides off the other end, she shows him about knots—and they begin again. The adult talks about the size, color, and feel of the beads but lets him choose which ones to string. □ When he is comfortable with the task, she watches from a distance while he makes the necklace. When he's ready to wear it, she admires the necklace as she ties it closed for him.

CHILD: The child will soon learn how to string and probably will be very serious about choosing just the right bead. He will be concerned with the beads one at a time and won't plan what his necklace will look like when it's finished. He may be happy with only one bead on a string but another time he won't stop until the string is full. □ This is an activity he can accomplish himself and feel good.about. And he'll be proud to wear the product when he's finished. The child will find things on his own to add to the box. This is an ongoing activity, and as he continues to have free choice over the months and years, he'll begin to work out patterns in his creations.

WHY GOAL: To help the child begin to use his hands and eyes together to string beads and other things. To help him choose for himself.

USES: Children develop confidence in themselves when their choices bring them satisfaction. Providing them with opportunities for successful selection is an important task of the adult.

87. Choosing with Beads

HOW You and your child can fill a box with small, pretty things that have a big hole in them—beads, shells, paper shapes, macaroni. You can put in some shoe laces. Let him make a necklace when he's in the mood. He gets to choose what he wants on it, and you get to admire it when he's through.

WHY To help the child begin to string things and to let him choose for himself

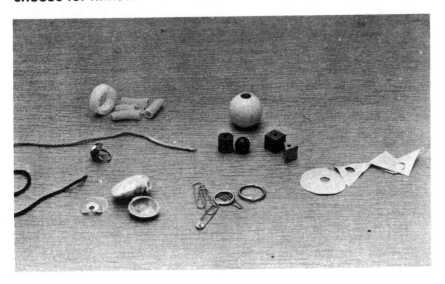

Safety note: Use of any items small enough to swallow should be well supervised.

88. In, Out, and Around

HOW ADULT: With a *box*, a small *object*, and a large piece of *paper* you can show the child the meaning of the words "in," "out," "around," "on top of." Show him first and then let him put the object in, take the object out, put the paper on top of, wrap the paper around. Also use words that help the child understand the place of things as you care for and talk with him:

> Your shirt is **in** the drawer.
> Dump the bugs **out** of the cup.
> Wrap it **around** your shoulders.
> Your bear is **on** the table.

☐ To help with other space relationships, play other games with him. Use a toy that clearly has a back and front (a truck) and a smaller toy (for the driver). You and the child can put the driver beside the truck, behind the truck, in front of the truck, under the truck. A made-up story about a driver and his truck makes it much more fun to move the driver around.

CHILD: The child will need to hear the words repeatedly in many situations before he understands for sure. It helps him to use toys that have a decided front or back or side. (It's hard to tell the front or side of a bowl or box.) If a story is told, the child will feel he is helping to tell it as he moves the toy around.

WHY GOAL: To frequently use words that show positions (prepositions). To provide ways for the child to see one object in relation to another.

USES: Understanding that words can not only name objects but can tell their positions and relationships is a significant step in the development of the child's language. Relationships help us string words and ideas together.

88. In, Out, and Around

HOW Think of some games to help your child with such special words as "in" and "on" and "under." Let him put his bear in the bed or under the bed. Use the words as you talk about his play: "hat on" . . . "kangaroo in" . . . "shoes under." Talk about your actions as you cuddle him: "arms around" . . . "kiss on the nose."

WHY To use words that can help your child learn about positions

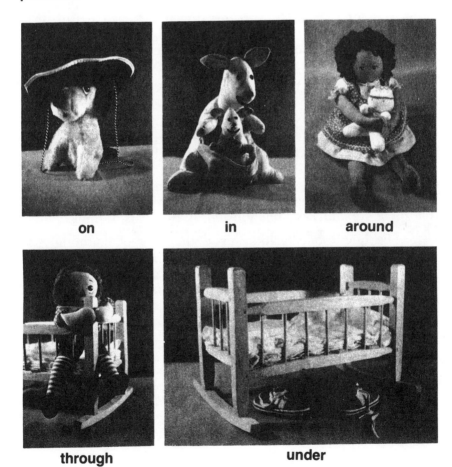

on in around

through under

89. Giving One to Each

HOW ADULT: When you're setting a table, ask the child to help. Show him how to put a napkin beside one plate. Give him just enough *napkins* and ask him to put one beside each plate. If he doesn't have enough to go around, go back with him to the places to see where he has put more than one. Ask if there is more than one there and explain that one can be taken away. ☐ This can be done with *spoons* or plastic *glasses*, also you can say "one" as he puts the things down or make a chant of "One for Daddy; one for Jean; one for Amy" as the child places the objects. You can help him with *cookies* at snacktime, *paper towels* at washing time, *flowers* picked for the family, *pictures* drawn for each person in a group, etc. Later you can count together as he gives out the things, but just to learn the sounds of the words. He's much too young to know clearly the meaning of the numbers.

CHILD: The child will like helping with grown-up jobs. He will not lay things down straight or always on the correct side. He will begin to see that words tell you how many, and after some time he will understand that to have just enough to go around he must use just one for each person. He will feel good about being a big help with a grown-up task.

WHY GOAL: To provide experience that will help the child know that there are limits and relationships in numbers of things.

USES: The one-to-one relationship is the basis of counting, and knowing how to allocate materials is a start in the process of planning. This understanding will be important to the child who in the future will live in a world conscious of the need for planning and conservation.

89. Giving One to Each

HOW Putting a spoon at each plate helps your child learn about numbers and planning. Give him just enough napkins or spoons or cookies, and let him give one to each person or place. Pick a flower to give to each member of the family. Help him to sort it out if he gives two or three together and runs short.

WHY To give the child some everyday experiences with numbers

90. Making a Fun Path

HOW ADULT: A path can be made for the child with things to step over or jump from or crawl through. Use a piece of *rope* as a guide if one is needed. Some things you might place along the path are a *cardboard box* opened at both ends, a small *stool or box* to climb on and jump off, a crumpled *towel* to step over. You can use whatever is at hand, keeping in mind the skills of the child. □ Change the path frequently, using some new things each time. Stay close by and you can help her by using space words: "You're going under the bench, over the paper," etc. You'll probably be unable to resist the fun of following the fun path with her. A room in the house can be used if outdoor space is unavailable. A string path can lead her through the door, around the chair, and under the table.

CHILD: The child will try most of the things but not always in the order they are laid out. If the adult plays follow the leader with her a few times, she will begin to see the order of things. (Some methodical children will be very strict with themselves about following the path exactly.) □ She'll like having a friend to play this game with her because they can play separately but still have fun together. If the path has new things added on different days, she'll be eager to try them.

WHY GOAL: To encourage the child's physical development. To use words that make her aware of space and position.

USES: Skill in using your body in space contributes to good health and creates recreational opportunities.

90. Making a Fun Path

HOW Set up a fun path of things the child can step over, crawl under, jump in, step on. Think about what she can do now and make it fun for her. Lay down some rope for her to follow from object to object. Sometimes act her age and follow as she leads.

WHY To encourage the child's physical development

91. Using Words for Time

HOW ADULT: As the child becomes more comfortable with words, make a point of using words about time. Say such things as: "After our story it will be time for a bath." "We will eat before you take your nap." "This morning when you were in the sandbox . . ." Don't expect the child to understand periods of time—just what's happening now or a little earlier or a little later. ☐ Say such things as "in a few minutes" or "at snack time" and the child will begin to have some idea of the meaning. By relating it to a familiar event, you give him a clue. If you say "next summer," it will have little meaning to him. But if you say "the next time we go to the beach," he will have a better idea, though he still may think that's tomorrow. A child might possibly remember a special event that happened some time ago, but he probably won't be sure if that was a long time ago or was yesterday.

CHILD: The child at this age has no concept of time as it is defined in the adult world by hours, weeks, and years. He can relate time only to what he is doing (for example, when the blocks are put away) or to a part of his day that is routine (lunchtime, for example). He begins to understand what it is the words are telling him long before he's able to use them correctly.

WHY GOAL: To use words that will help him begin to understand time as a relationship.

USES: Words about time give the child a tool for sequencing and predicting. The present moment can take on more meaning as the child gradually learns to look backward and forward in time.

91. Using Words for Time

HOW Begin to use words about time. Talk about "after our story" or "when Mommy comes home." Help him understand by relating the words to a time he knows, such as lunchtime. Learning will be fun for you both.

WHY To help the child begin to understand that words can tell him when things will happen

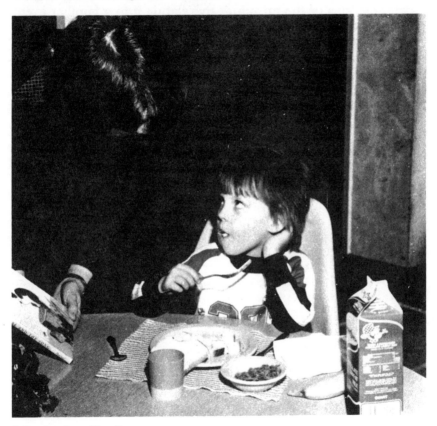

"after lunch we'll . . ."

92. Listening and Supporting

HOW ADULT: Listening to the child as he begins to express his needs takes a lot of patience and a strong desire to understand. When he comes to you with a need, take his hand and go with him to see what his language is inadequate to explain. Then help him with the words. "You did need help with the buggy. I'm glad you came to tell me." Continue to help him think ahead and plan his own needs. □ Sometimes he can't show you what he needs; then you support him by listening to the few words he does say and using what you know of his ways to read between the lines. "Book" may mean he wants comfort and needs to cuddle in your lap like he does when you read; it may mean his book is out of reach; or it may be he saw a dog and wants to find the picture he remembers in a book. Stay calm and do the best you can. Let your response be at a level that corresponds to the need. Obviously there are times when you must act quickly and decisively. But sometimes a more leisurely, less intense response is quite adequate. Your level of response gives the child some measure against which to gauge the importance of his various needs.

CHILD: The child has many needs at this age of great exploration. He has some difficulty in knowing what they are. At times he knows only that he needs something. At other times he knows what he needs but doesn't know how to tell anybody else. □ He can be remarkably patient when the grown-ups don't understand, but sometimes he has no patience at all, resorting to yelling and crying. With your support he will keep trying words until he finds the right ones.

WHY GOAL: To listen sympathetically and creatively to the child when he expresses his needs.

USES: Supporting the child in his expressed needs lets him know he's worthy of attention and encourages him to be more conscious of others' needs.

92. Listening and Supporting

HOW Listen to your child when he tells you what he needs. You're helping him to see that he's important when you pay special attention to what he says. He doesn't have enough words yet to say exactly what he wants. You can read between the lines and usually figure it out. Work at it together and support each other until he knows the words.

WHY To listen to the child when he expresses his needs . . . later this may help him become a good listener

93. Pairing and Sorting Pictures

HOW ADULT: Groups can be made up of things that look alike, act alike, are used alike, etc. You can help the child see what makes things alike by using pictures. □ Show her *two pictures that are just alike*. Point out details in one picture and encourage the child to find those same things in the other picture. Look at some more pairs, then mix up two sets and let her pair the ones that "look alike." Identical pictures can be cut from two copies of the same magazine advertisement. □ Another time show her a collection of *pictures of items that have a common use*, such as things to eat with. Say something like, "This is a spoon. We eat with it. Can you find another picture of something we use when we eat?" Choose together all the pictures that are "alike"—that is, that are used in eating. Other categories that the child can understand are things you wear, people, toys, and animals. (A mail-order catalog is an excellent source for such pictures.) □ Ask her why a picture doesn't belong in a particular group. If she answers in a word or two—"don't eat," you can expand the idea: "That's right, that's a shoe. You don't eat shoes, you wear them." She may tease you and pretend not to know after she becomes sure of herself, and you'll find yourself enjoying her as much as she's enjoying the game.

CHILD: If the objects are things she knows, she may name them but not be able to tell why one is different. With hints from the adult she is able to tell enough so that the adult knows she can see the differences. She may choose a category and want the adult to find the things for it.

WHY GOAL: To help the child learn that things can be grouped by the way they look or the way they are used or in many other ways. To help the child begin to express ideas.

USES: The child can more quickly learn new objects if they are a part of a familiar group. For example, "It's something to eat" gives her a lot of information about a new fruit.

93. Pairing and Sorting Pictures

HOW Show her two pictures that are just alike. Point out how they are alike. Look at some more pairs. Then mix two sets of them. Hold up one picture and ask, "Can you find one like this?" Later, help her to make groups such as things to eat, things to play with, people, or animals. Also encourage her to group the pictures in any way she wishes. You will get to know her better as she sorts by her own impressions.

WHY To help the child group pictures and notice many kinds of similarities

94. What's Gone?

HOW Adult: When you are cleaning up from a playtime, leave *two things* on the table or floor. Talk about what they are, name them, and have the child name them. Ask the child to close her eyes; remove one of the things, and have her open her eyes and tell you what is gone. If she can't remember, put the object back and repeat the game. When she can play the game well, you can use more than two things or sometimes let her play it with another child, showing them things laid out on a tray. □ Play it in a little different way as you care for her. At bathtime show her the towel and soap and ask her what's missing. If she doesn't say washcloth, ask a leading question about what she usually takes to her bath. See if she misses her spoon from her lunch tray when you ask what's missing. If she doesn't seem to notice missing things, make a point in the next few days of calling her attention to objects she uses in a particular situation. Then try the game again. Don't forget to talk about the family: "I'm here, you're here, who's gone?"

Child: When you first play this game, she may not remember the missing item. The game will give her a reason to begin to notice more carefully. She may begin to notice (before the adult asks) that her spoon is not there and say so. Some children like to lead the game and hide the spoon in their lap to see if the adult notices. Often they can't wait to share the fun and will say, "Spoon's gone."

WHY Goal: To encourage the child to pay attention to her surroundings, to notice things, and to remember things that were there.

Uses: Knowing what is gone is a sign of a growing memory—and memory is used in many important mental processes.

94. What's Gone?

HOW When you're putting away toys, leave two. Show them to the child and let her tell you what they are. While she hides her eyes, take one away. Have her open her eyes and tell you what's gone. Give her a big hug when she tells you. Hide your eyes and let her take one away. Maybe you'll get a big hug if you're right.

WHY To encourage the child to notice things and to remember things that were there

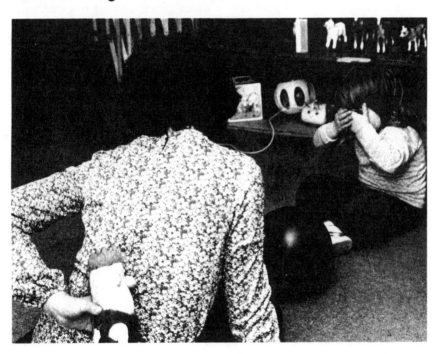

95. Cutting and Pasting

HOW Adult: When a child is using her fingers and wrists well, she can begin to use *scissors*. Make sure that she has children's scissors and sit with her while she uses them. Let her hold them in the way that is comfortable for her. Show her with another pair how the blades open and shut. □ To keep her interested, help her by holding a long, thin strip of *firm paper* in such a way that she can snip it. Let her know you're happy about the little snips as well as the bigger ones that separate the paper into two pieces. When she wants to hold the paper, let her try, but help her again if she can't manage it. Then give her a wider piece and let her cut snips in the edge like fringe. □ The scraps that she cuts might be saved for pasting. Show her how to put some *paste* on a scrap and stick it to a bigger sheet of paper. If she's interested in the paste itself, let her explore it by tasting and feeling. Be careful not to expect her to cut on lines or cut out shapes. Let her be the judge of what she can do. You can encourage her by supporting her efforts.

Child: At first the child will be interested in making the blades move. She may hold a handle in each hand and snip them together just to see and hear them. She's finding out how they work. To begin with, she'll hold the scissors awkwardly and not be able to cut much except snips. She may be satisfied to make a cut or two, but later she'll keep right on snipping all the way around the paper. She's enjoying the process of cutting and pasting and is not "making something."

WHY Goal: To provide a successful experience with scissors and paste. To help the child improve her fine motor skills.

Uses: Children need to know how to use the basic tools of their culture. She will need to know how to use scissors throughout her life, and the fine motor control she develops may contribute to many future hand activities.

95. Cutting and Pasting

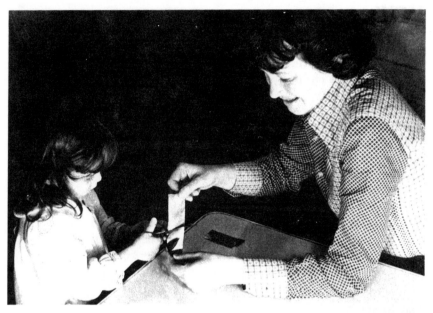

HOW Don't be afraid to give your young child scissors when the right time comes. Make sure they're safe ones. Give her a chance to handle them and see how they work. Then hold a strip of paper while she begins with little snips. Make it a sharing time and stay with her while she learns. You'll feel comfortable when you see how well she handles them in this planned experience.

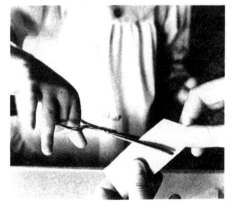

WHY To let the child have fun while she's improving her hand skills

96. Helping Him Help Himself

HOW ADULT: The adult can help the child become a more independent table companion. When it's possible, she puts some of the food to be served in *small bowls* with soup spoons. She invites the child to serve his own plate. Placing the serving bowl in a good position for the child, she shows him how to use the serving spoon. She allows him to choose the size serving he wants but guides him by suggesting that he take some now and have more later if he still wants it. If he manages to get only a small bit on his plate, the adult goes with the decision and lets him eat that before offering him more. □ The child can serve his own milk if the adult encourages him by providing equipment that is easy to handle. In a *small pitcher* the adult puts just enough milk for the child's cup. Then there's not as much to spill. (At first the adult might hold the cup for him.) As he becomes more skillful, she shows him how to hold his cup with one hand and the pitcher with the other. The adult expects spills and goes to the table with a large supply of patience. □ The needs of the whole family or the day-care group help to determine which mealtimes can be most conveniently used for this learning experience. Self-service is not appropriate all the time.

CHILD: The child is likely to be a little messy at first, but that is just because it's new and he's excited and not very skilled. He'll regulate the amount when it is no longer a novelty to serve himself. (Some children actually eat better after they've begun to serve themselves.) □ When pouring, he may not notice how full the cup is getting, or he may pour before he gets the pitcher over the cup or may set the pitcher down without making sure it's safe. There are a lot of things he has to remember to do, but most children are so pleased with themselves that they keep trying.

WHY GOAL: To arrange things so the child can (at least partly) serve his own plate at the table and to allow him to make some choices about what he eats.

USES: Skill in choosing and serving are used at mealtime throughout life.

96. Helping Him Help Himself

HOW Patience and planning help you help the young child serve himself at meals. When you can, use small serving bowls he can handle. Put only a little milk in a small pitcher for him to pour. Be ready with lots of patience for the messiness that has to happen. You'll probably find he eats better when he has served himself.

WHY To allow the child to increase his independence with choices about what he eats

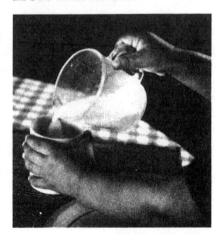

97. What Would Happen If . . .

HOW ADULT: To help your child know about the order of things, play a game with him about disorder in time or space. This helps him to think what the logical order should be and to exercise his imagination. Play a game with the child as you live with him during the day. □ Pretend to make "mistakes" in some common activities: zip his coat up before he puts his arm in the sleeve; hold his glass upside down as you start to tip the milk carton to pour. The two of you can have a good laugh as you correct the situation. Later, ask him, "What would happen if: you zipped your coat before you put it on? you put your shoes on before your socks? your bowl was upside down when you poured your cereal? you locked the door before you went out?" □ You can help him in the telling by repeating back to him in a sentence the words he says to you and by saying what must happen first: "First you unzip the coat—next you put it on." "You unlock the door—then you open it." Listen for the words "first, then, next, until" and congratulate him when you hear them in his speech.

CHILD: One or two words may be all the child says at first but they tell the adult that he's figured out her riddle. Later he'll repeat the sentence the adult makes from his one-word answer, and even later will answer in sentences of his own. He is beginning to be able to imagine things, and you may occasionally get a clever, imaginative answer to a "what if . . ." question.

WHY GOAL: To help the child understand what must happen first and to learn the words to say it.

USES: Understanding the necessary order in which things happen is a basic step in reasoning.

97. What Would Happen If ...

HOW Pretend some topsy-turvy experiences with your child. See how he figures a way to handle them. Ask, "What would happen if . . . you put your shoes on before your socks . . . your glass is upside down when I start to pour your milk?" Have a good time acting some of these situations out. You might be pleasantly surprised at his understanding. Help him with words as he shows or tells you what he'd do.

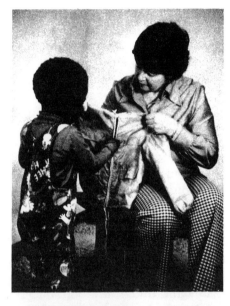

WHY To help the child think about what must happen first

98. Running and Walking Together

HOW ADULT: When the child is outside and ready to play with someone, he can be shown some special ways of moving. The adult can exaggerate her walking steps and say, "See, I am walking." Then she suddenly starts to run and says, "I'm running." She can go back and take the child's hand, and they can play the game together. They can agree to walk to a certain spot, then run from that point on. Using the words "run" and "walk" helps the child remember the difference. □ The child does a lot of natural running at this age, but he lives in a world where he's always being told "walk, don't run." Playing at running helps him to realize that running is okay, but it can't be done just anyplace. The game also helps him know what running actually is and isn't. □ The adult will be able to invent some actions that make it even more special. Running in a circle, running like a horse with knees and head up high, or walking ever so slowly each provide a new kind of experience for the two to share. The adult listens for these words "run, walk, fast, slow" in the child's talk and gives them particular praise.

CHILD: The child will like playing a large-muscle game with the adult and will soon know which actions to do from the words. He may want to choose when to run and be the one to call the signals. Sometimes he'll run around in every direction and be silly and run when he's supposed to be walking and just generally have a great time. Perhaps knowing he can share running outdoors will make it a little easier to walk indoors when he's asked to.

WHY GOAL: To share some good times with your child while he's developing his skill in running and moving.

USES: Becoming aware is the first step in being able to do something with an intentional plan. Moving quickly from running to walking makes him aware of what's happening to his body and consequently how better to direct it.

98. Running and Walking Together

HOW Remember how it felt to run freely when you were a child? You often have to say, "Walk, don't run" to your child—because you want him to be safe. But sometimes go out and play running games with him. Run fast, walk slow, gallop like a horse, shuffle like an elephant. Run where he leads you.

WHY To share some good times with your child while he's learning to move well

99. Telling Family Stories

HOW ADULT: Collect some *pictures* from magazines and catalogs that can stand for members of the family or the members of the day-care group. Glue them to *popsicle sticks* to make little puppets. Make up a story about the family or the day-care group and let the children move the puppets around to act it out. Include some things that really happened and make up some imaginary things. □ Let the child tell part of the story as you ask, "What do you think she did then?" or "How did it make you feel?" Talk about the adults so the child can experience them as people with feelings and needs, too. Later, find some photos of the child when she was a baby and tell stories about what she did. Tell her what you liked about her then and what you like now. □ Leave the puppets or pictures (perhaps in a little box as their house) for her to play with sometimes. We hope she might make up her own story to tell you or to tell when she plays with other children.

CHILD: The child has no formal understanding of the time between now and then. But she loves to hear about "When I was a baby." She will begin to ask questions about whether she did certain things or where she slept. She has fun choosing the people to represent the family, though the reasons for her choices may not always be clear to the adult. Handling the puppets helps her to see the family as a group with the members each being a part.

WHY GOAL: To help the child know herself better, and to help her see her secure place in a group.

USES: Feeling she's an important part of a family or other group helps the child have a secure base of operation from which to move into wider circles of her society.

99. Telling Family Stories

HOW Collect some pictures that look like the people in your family. Paste them on sticks to make puppets. Tell a story about your family and let the children move the puppets to act it out. Let them tell part of the story. Talk about what they did as little babies (and what they might do when they're older). Tell who they did things with. It will help them begin to see what being a family is all about.

WHY To help the child see her place in relation to others

100. I See Something That Is...

HOW ADULT: When the child can answer questions about "how it's used," the adult can start a simple version of I Spy (with her and maybe a couple of her friends or classmates). He gives two hints: one, the color of the object; two, what the object is used for. "I see something that is red. You drink from it." □ He plays the game by facing in the general direction of the object and asking the children to go and touch it if they see it. He repeats the clue often. When a child finds the object, the adult says, "Yes, this is red. You can drink from it. You listened very carefully!" He lets the child name it if she can. □ If a child chooses the wrong object, he says, "This is red. But you can't drink from it. Let's look some more." He then repeats the clues. If the game seems too hard, the adult places three things together on a table in front of the children and asks for one of these things. Some children find it hard just to touch the object; they want to bring the object and show it to the adult. That's okay if the adult is careful to ask for things the child can get and carry easily. The game stops when the children's interest stops.

CHILD: Playing a game with rules will be fun, but it may take a few tries for the children to understand their part. When they look for something, some children will begin by guessing wildly, but as the game goes on, they begin to think more carefully before running to touch just any object. When a child touches the wrong thing, she's not likely to be discouraged. When the clues are repeated, she's off again.

WHY GOAL: To help the child listen to directions. To help the child consider two aspects of an object.

USES: Considering two features of an object requires the child to do a two-step evaluation to identify it. She must weigh both considerations and come to a conclusion as she will do with many evaluations all of her life.

100. I See Something That Is...

HOW Play a small-child version of "I Spy." Ask the child to find an object. Give her two clues—one about color and one about how it's used: "I see something red that you drink from." Tell her how smart she was to find it. Let her use the object before you go on with the game.

WHY To help the child consider two aspects of an object

BIBLIOGRAPHY

1. For Parents and Day-Care Centers

Gordon, Ira. *Baby Learning Through Baby Play: A Parent Guide for the First Two Years.* New York: St. Martin's Press, 1970.

————. *Baby to Parent, Parent to Baby: A Guide to Loving and Learning in a Child's First Year.* New York: St. Martin's Press, 1978.

Gordon, Ira; Guinagh, Barry; and Jester, J. Emile. *Child Learning Through Child Play: Learning Activities for Two- and Three-Year-Olds.* New York: St. Martin's Press, 1972.

Painter, Genevieve. *Teach Your Baby.* New York: Simon and Schuster, 1971.

Segal, Marilyn. *From Birth to One Year.* Rolling Hills Estates, Calif.: B. L. Winch and Associates, 1974.

Segal, Marilyn, and Adcock, Don. *From One to Two Years.* Rolling Hills Estates, Calif.: B. L. Winch and Associates, 1976.

Segner, Leslie, and Patterson, Charlotte. *Ways to Help Babies Grow and Learn: Activities for Infant Education.* Denver: World Press, 1970.

2. Especially for Parents

Caplan, Frank, ed. *The Parenting Advisor.* Garden City, N.Y.: Anchor Press Doubleday, 1977.

Leach, Penelope, *Your Baby and Child from Birth to Age Five.* New York: Alfred A. Knopf, 1978.

Marzollo, Jean. *Supertot, Creative Learning Activities for Children One to Three and Sympathetic Advice for Their Parents.* New York: Harper and Row, 1976.

3. Especially for Day-Care Centers

Herbert-Jackson, Emily; O'Brien, Marion; Porterfield, Jan; and Risley, Todd R. *The Infant Center, A Complete Guide to Organizing and Managing Infant Day Care.* Baltimore: University Park Press, 1977.

Honig, Alice, and Lally, J. Ronald. *Infant Caregiving: A Design for Training.* New York: Open Family Press, 1974.

Keister, Mary Elizabeth. *"The Good Life" for Infants and Toddlers.* Washington, D.C.: National Association for the Education of Young Children, 1970.

Willis, Ann, and Ricciuti, Henry. *A Good Beginning for Babies, Guidelines for Group Care.* Washington, D.C.: National Association for the Education of Young Children, 1975.

4. Adult Reference on Infancy and Child Development

Braga, Laurie and Joseph. *Learning and Growing: A Guide to Child Development.* Englewood Cliffs, N.J.: Prentice-Hall, 1975.

Brazelton, T. Berry. *Infants and Mothers: Differences in Development.* New York: Dell Publishing Co., 1969.

Brazelton, T. Berry. *Toddlers and Parents: A Declaration of Independence.* New York: Dell Publishing Co., 1974.

Caplan, Frank, ed. *The First Twelve Months of Life, Your Baby's Growth Month by Month.* New York: Grosset and Dunlap, 1973.

Caplan, Frank, ed. *The Second Twelve Months of Life.* New York: Grosset and Dunlap, 1977.

Church, Joseph. *Understanding Your Child from Birth to Three, A Guide to Your Child's Psychological Development*. New York: Random House, 1973.

White, Burton L. *The First Three Years of Life*. Englewood Cliffs, N.J.: Prentice-Hall, 1975.

5. Child References on Infancy

Showers, Paul. *The Moon Walker*. Garden City, N.Y.: Doubleday and Co., 1975.

Stein, Sara Bonnett. *That New Baby, An Open Family Book for Parents and Children Together*. New York: Walker and Company, 1974.

6. References Used for Checklists in this Book

Alpern, G. D., and Boll, T. J., *Developmental Profile*. Indianapolis: Psychological Developmental Publications, 1972.

Bayley, N. *Bayley Scales of Infant Development*. New York: Psychological Corporation, 1969.

Doll, E. A. *Preschool Attainment Record*. Circle Pines, Minn.: American Guidance Service, 1966.

Koontz, C. W. *Koontz Child Development Program:* Training Activities for the First 48 Months. Los Angeles: Western Psychological Services, 1974.